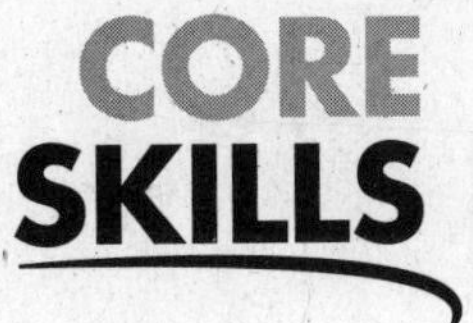

# Test Preparation

## Grade 8



Printed in the U.S.A.

ISBN 978-0-544-26860-9

1 2 3 4 5 6 7 8 9 10 0982 22 21 20 19 18 17 16 15 14 13

4500438435 A B C D E F G

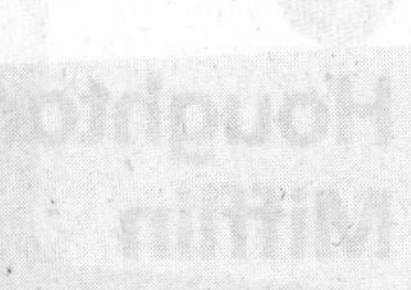

Dear Parent or Educator,

Welcome to *Core Skills: Test Preparation*. You have selected a book that will help your child develop the skills he or she needs to succeed on standardized tests.

Although testing can be a source of anxiety for children, this book will give your child the preparation and practice that he or she needs to feel better prepared and more confident when taking a standardized test. Research shows that children who are acquainted with the scoring format of standardized tests score higher on those tests. Students also score higher when they practice and understand the skills and strategies needed to take standardized tests. The subject areas and concepts presented in this book are typically found on standardized tests at this grade level.

To best help your child, please consider the following suggestions:

- Provide a quiet place to work.
- Go over the directions and the sample exercises together.
- Review the strategy tips.
- Reassure your child that the practice tests are not "real" tests.
- Encourage your child to do his or her best.
- Check the lesson when it is complete.
- Go over the answers and note improvements as well as problems.

If your child expresses anxiety about taking a test or completing these lessons, help him or her understand what causes the stress. Then, talk about ways to eliminate anxiety. Above all, enjoy this time you spend with your child. He or she will feel your support, and test scores will improve as success in test taking is experienced.

Help your child maintain a positive attitude about taking a standardized test. Let your child know that each test provides an opportunity to shine.

Sincerely,

The Educators and Staff of
Houghton Mifflin Harcourt

P.S. You might want to visit our website at **www.hmhco.com** for more test preparation materials as well as additional review of content areas.

# Core Skills: Test Preparation

# GRADE 8

## Contents

Dear Student,
Sometime during the school year, you will be taking standardized tests. This book can help you prepare to take such tests.
Here are some suggestions for using these practice tests and for taking the "real" tests.

**DO:**

- Listen to or read all the directions.
- Read the **Try This** strategy tips, do the **Sample** items, and then look at **Think It Through** to check your answer before you begin each lesson.
- Look over the entire test or section before you begin.
- Stay calm, concentrate on the test, and clear your mind of things that have nothing to do with the test.
- Read all the answer choices before choosing the one that you think is best.
- Make sure the number you fill in on the answer sheet matches the question number on the test page.
- Trust your first instinct when answering each question.
- Answer the easy questions first, then go back and work on the ones you aren't sure about.
- Take all the time you are allowed.

**DON'T:**

- Look ahead to another question until you complete the one you're working on.
- Spend too much time on one question.
- Rush.
- Worry if others finish while you are still working.
- Change an answer unless you are really sure it should be changed.

**Remember to do your best!**

# Standardized Test Content Areas

The following skills are tested on most standardized exams. These same skills are included in *Core Skills: Test Preparation, Grade 8.*

## Reading Skills

*Identifying synonyms

*Identifying passage details, the main idea, sequence of events, genre, cause and effect

*Recognizing supporting details

*Analyzing character

*Drawing conclusions

Distinguishing between fact and opinion

*Using context to determine word meaning

*Identifying the author's purpose

Determining tone

*Using definitional phrases to determine word meanings

## Language Skills

*Determining topic relevance

*Identifying the correct use of general reference materials

*Interpreting dictionary entries

Using a table of contents and an index of a book to locate information

*Identifying clearly written sentences

*Determining appropriate topic sentences and supporting sentences

*Identifying extraneous information within a paragraph

*Identifying correctly applied grammar

*Identifying correct capitalization and punctuation

*Recognizing misspelled words

*Identifying correct spellings of words

## Mathematics Skills

Comparing and ordering fractions

Identifying equivalent fractions, alternatives of fractions, mixed numbers, and decimals

Identifying integers on a number line and those greater or less than a negative integer

*Identifying place value, primes, composites, numbers in scientific notation, powers, and square roots

*Solving inequalities and linear equations and evaluating linear expressions

Identifying the algebraic expression and meaning in words of an algebraic expression

*Identifying the output of functions and missing elements in numeric patterns

*Solving problems involving rate and proportion

+Predicting outcomes and using a statistical sampling to predict outcomes

+Determining combinations and permutations

Extrapolating from multiple bar graphs

+Reading and interpreting frequency tables, stem-and-leaf plots, tally charts, scattergrams, and histograms

+Identifying probabilities and determining the mean

Classifying polyhedrons

*Identifying coordinates, transformations, radius, diameter, and parallel and perpendicular lines

+Calculating volume of rectangular prisms, circumference, and area of circles and irregular figures

Converting between units of measurement within the same system

Measuring length and estimating angles

+Determining measurements indirectly from similar figures and scale drawings

*Using estimation in operations with compatible whole numbers, decimals, money, fractions, percents, and in clustering

Identifying reasonableness

*Using problem-solving strategies and identifying missing information in problems

*Demonstrating the ability to add, subtract, multiply, and divide

*Applying addition, subtraction, multiplication, and division concepts to word problems

*Aligns to Grade 8 Common Core State Standards.

+Extension: Reading and Language Skills align to Grade 9 Common Core State Standards.
Mathematics Skills align to Algebra 1 Common Core Standards.

# Listening Scripts

These scripts accompany the listening portions of the lessons and tests found in Unit 7 on pages 80–83 and in Unit 12 on pages 117 and 118. Before beginning the test, work the sample question with your child and discuss the correct answer. In all listening lessons and tests, give your child time to respond before reading the next question. You may read these items twice if needed.

## UNIT 7: LISTENING

### Understanding Word Meanings, p. 82

Look at Sample A. I will read a sentence and the four answer choices. You will find the word that best completes the sentence. Listen carefully.

She chose a **complicated** experiment for her science project. **Complicated** means —
**A** comforting … **B** simple … **C** difficult …
**D** frightening. Darken the circle for the word that best completes the sentence. (Discuss the question and answer as needed.)

Now you will answer numbers 1 through 10. Listen carefully to the sentence and the four answer choices. Then darken the circle for the correct answer.

1. Her lack of exceptional swimming skills was a **hindrance** to making the swim team. A hindrance is — **A** an assistance … **B** an obstacle … **C** a recovery … **D** an entertainment.
2. Why was your answer so **evasive?** Something that is evasive is — **F** unclear … **G** direct … **H** misleading … **J** specific.
3. The mother was concerned about her daughter's **aggressive** behavior. *Aggressive* means — **A** gentle … **B** hostile … **C** perturbed … **D** confused.
4. What will be the **consequence** of his actions? A consequence is a — **F** description … **G** cause … **H** prescription … **J** result.
5. She was **elated** about her new job. *Elated* means — **A** happy … **B** disappointed … **C** unhappy … **D** depressed.
6. Courtney knew that Rebecca was a **formidable** opponent. *Formidable* means — **F** easy … **G** impressive … **H** unimpressive … **J** inviting.
7. We continued to play tennis after the rains **diminished.** *Diminished* means — **A** increased … **B** ended … **C** decreased … **D** strengthened.
8. She arranged to have a shelf for **miscellaneous** items. *Miscellaneous* means — **F** assorted … **G** similar … **H** specific … **J** unusual.
9. The people **jostled** one another as they tried to get the best view of the president. To be jostled is to be — **A** stopped … **B** helped … **C** tripped … **D** shoved.
10. Is this an **authentic** painting of that artist? To be authentic is to be — **F** ancient … **G** valuable … **H** false … **J** genuine.

### Building Listening Skills, p. 83

Look at Sample A. I will read a passage and then ask a question. You will choose the best answer to the question. Listen carefully.

> The most important thing for gardeners to consider is the quality of the soil. Fertilizer or compost will add nutrients to the soil and help plants grow and bloom profusely. If the same soil is used from one year to the next, the soil will be stripped of nutrients and will be unable to help plants grow.

This passage would probably be found in — **A** an advertisement … **B** a gardening book … **C** a novel … **D** a fashion magazine. Darken the circle for the correct answer. (Discuss the question and answer as needed.)

Now you will practice answering more questions about stories that you hear. Find number 1. Listen carefully to the passage and the question. Then darken the circle for the correct answer. You will answer four questions.

After nearly a year of construction, the Bell Memorial Gym was opened on Friday, November 12. On hand to witness the proceedings was Karen Bell, whose generous donation made the new gym possible. Also attending the ceremony were Principal Butala, teachers, coaches, and at least five hundred students.

Those attending the opening admired the gym's size and equipment. Mr. Lester Owens, coach of the basketball team, was especially pleased with the good floor and new hoops. "We should win a lot of games this year," he said. Principal Butala expressed how pleased she was with the results. "The new gym will benefit all of the McKinley School students," she said. "Dances, games, assemblies, and special events can all be held in a more pleasant environment. The education of all students will be enhanced by this new addition to the school."

1. What did Coach Owens especially like about the gym? **A** the dances that could be held there … **B** the new floor … **C** the equipment … **D** the pleasant environment.
2. All of the following will probably be held in the gym except — **F** tests … **G** games … **H** dances … **J** assemblies.
3. Karen Bell is — **A** the school principal … **B** the person who donated money for the new gym … **C** a teacher … **D** the school basketball coach.
4. Where would this selection probably be found? **F** in an encyclopedia … **G** in a magazine … **H** in a school newspaper … **J** in a textbook.

Now find number 5. Listen to the passage. You will answer four questions.

The Olympic Games originated in Greece before 1400 B.C. Many games and festivals were held at that time to honor the Greek gods and goddesses. The Olympic Games especially honored Zeus, the king of the gods. When the Roman Empire conquered Greece, the games lost their religious significance. The Olympics were discontinued in A.D. 394 and were not held for about 1,500 years. The first modern games took place in 1896 in Athens, Greece. Women first competed in the modern games in 1900. Today athletes from all over the world compete for medals at the Olympic Games, which are held in different cities around the world.

5. Originally the Olympic Games were held to — **A** please the Romans … **B** give athletes a chance to compete … **C** raise money for athletic clubs … **D** honor Greek gods and goddesses.
6. Where did the Olympic Games originate? **F** in Rome … **G** in England … **H** in Greece … **J** in the United States.
7. For about how many years were the Olympic Games discontinued? **A** 400 years … **B** 1500 years … **C** 100 years … **D** 1,200 years.
8. In what year did women first compete in the modern games? **F** 1777 … **G** 1896 … **H** 1900 … **J** 1929.

Now find number 9. Listen to the passage. You will answer two questions.

Here are three easy steps for planting a tree — a good way to clean the air, provide a home for birds, and make the world more beautiful.

**Step 1:** Choose a good spot for the tree — not too close to a building, other trees, or telephone wires. Dig a two-foot-deep hole with sloping sides.

**Step 2:** Pick up the tree by the root ball, not the trunk, and set it in the hole. Then fill the hole with dirt around the root ball. When the hole is a little more than half full, fill the hole with water and stir the mud with your shovel. This will settle the soil and remove air pockets. Finish filling in the hole with dirt.

**Step 3:** Place mulch — or leaves, straw, or bark — around the tree. Water the tree and step back to admire your work!

9. Mulch can be all of the following except — **A** bark … **B** dirt … **C** straw … **D** leaves.
10. What is the first step in planting a tree? **F** dig a deep hole … **G** choose a good spot for the tree … **H** choose a young tree … **J** add mulch to the soil.

## Test, pp. 84–85

In this test you will use the listening skills we have practiced in this unit. This test is divided into two parts. For each part there is a sample exercise. Look at Sample A. I will read a sentence and the four answer choices. You will find the word that best completes the sentence. Listen carefully.

The students **compiled** their information in a pamphlet to be distributed to the entire school. **Compile** means to — **A** illustrate … **B** identify … **C** repeat … **D** put together. Darken the circle for the word that best completes the sentence.

You should have darkened the circle for D, put together, because *to compile* means to put together.

Now find number 1. We will do numbers 1 through 13. Listen carefully to the sentence and the four answer choices. Then darken the circle for the correct answer.

1. The designer needed to be **accurate** in his measurements. To be accurate is to be — **A** exact … **B** jumbled … **C** wrong … **D** exaggerated.
2. The children were in a **giddy** mood during the party. To be giddy is to be — **F** serious … **G** silly … **H** steady … **J** weary.
3. On our hike we saw a bobcat **maul** a bird. *Maul* means — **A** mangle … **B** spy … **C** play with … **D** observe.
4. What can you do to **accelerate** the sale of this product? To accelerate is to — **F** decrease … **G** stop … **H** increase …**J** advertise.
5. I do not **deem** it necessary to have a party. *Deem* means — **A** make … **B** like … **C** suppose … **D** consider.
6. We listened to our grandmother **recollect** her childhood experiences. To recollect is to — **F** organize … **G** classify … **H** laugh about … **J** remember.
7. The **smirk** on his face angered his parents. A smirk is a kind of — **A** color … **B** mark … **C** smile … **D** wound.
8. Margaret maintained a **neutral** position in her friends' argument. *Neutral* means — **F** unbiased … **G** close-minded … **H** colorful … **J** biased.
9. The mother tried to quiet her **obnoxious** child. To be obnoxious is to be — **A** charming … **B** annoying … **C** delightful … **D** tolerable.
10. You need to be aware of a cat's **temperament** before you bring it home. *Temperament* means — **F** climate … **G** anger … **H** background … **J** nature.
11. The firefighters ordered the people to **vacate** the building. To vacate is to — **A** leave … **B** fix … **C** enter … **D** occupy.
12. Mr. Reynolds was **optimistic** that his business would succeed. To be optimistic is to be — **F** hopeless … **G** unconvinced … **H** hopeful … **J** pessimistic.
13. It is difficult to set up a budget if you have too many **variable** costs. To be variable is to be — **A** changeable … **B** constant … **C** expensive … **D** unchangeable.

Now turn to page 85.

Look at Sample B. I will read a passage and then ask a question. You will choose the best answer to the question. Listen carefully.

> Spiders use their silk threads to spin webs. The webs are used for catching prey. Spiders also use their silk to make cocoons for their eggs. Many spiders spin a single line of silk wherever they go. They use this "lifeline" to escape from enemies.

What do spiders use to escape from their enemies? **A** a single line of silk … **B** a cocoon … **C** spider eggs … **D** prey. Darken the circle for the correct answer.

You should have darkened the circle for A, a single line of silk, because the passage stated that spiders spin a single line of silk. The passage referred to the line of silk as the "lifeline" to escape from enemies.

Find number 14. Listen carefully to the passage and the question. Then darken the circle for the correct answer. You will answer four questions.

> In Salisbury, England, there stands a group of large, rough stones placed together thousands of years ago. This ancient monument is called Stonehenge. No one knows why it was built. Some of the stones were probably transported from Wales, about 300 miles away. Over the years, many of the stones have fallen or have been removed. But from the position of the remaining stones, scientists can guess what the monument once looked like. Scientists are trying to discover the purpose of Stonehenge. Many believe it was used as a calendar to predict the phases of the moon and the seasons.

**14.** The stones that make up Stonehenge — **F** all came from Salisbury, England … **G** are all intact … **H** might have been transported from Wales … **J** were small and smooth.

**15.** Which of the following statements accurately describes scientists' knowledge of Stonehenge? **A** Scientists can only guess what the monument once looked like … **B** The monument has been unchanged over the years … **C** Scientists know exactly how the monument was used … **D** Scientists know why it was built.

**16.** Stonehenge is — **F** a building … **G** an ancient monument … **H** an ancient city … **J** a quarry.

**17.** You could visit Stonehenge if you were traveling in — **A** Wales … **B** Ireland … **C** Asia … **D** England.

Now find number 18. Listen to the passage. You will answer three questions.

The following notice was printed in the local newspaper:

Won't you help the homeless? With your help, many families will no longer be homeless. The city has set up a plan to provide housing for many families. These houses will have basic appliances and furniture, but much more is needed. Please search your closets, basements, and attics for household items and clothing that you no longer use. Items will be collected at the Dexter School Gym from July 26th through August 5th. The gym will be open Monday through Friday from 5:00 P.M. until 7:00 P.M. and Saturday and Sunday from 9:00 A.M. until 12 noon. PLEASE HELP!

**18.** To attract attention, this notice — **F** talks about one homeless family … **G** asks for money … **H** offers money for donated items … **J** asks a question.

**19.** What will the city provide for some homeless families? **A** a house with some furniture … **B** a house with everything a family will need for a year … **C** an empty house … **D** a house that will need many improvements.

**20.** What does the notice ask people to do with the items they collect? **F** call the city to pick up the items … **G** give the items to friends and neighbors … **H** bring the items to the school gym … **J** give the items directly to a homeless family.

Now look at number 21. Listen to the poem. You will answer four questions.

I live in the part of the country
where the little house was built.
Pioneers who first viewed this land,
Saw it as a sea of grass.
When the wind blows the grass,
It ripples like ocean waves,
Not large enough to splash.
Standing in the middle of the prairie,
I feel like a single blade,
Coaxed to move like all the rest.
Untouched prairie grass feels like bear fur,
Enticing me to reach out and pet it.
The soil of the prairie is dark and fertile.
Rotting roots feed plants and flowers, wild.
Asters, goldenrod, and sunflowers play in the prairie.
Adding their own spatter of color to the embracing landscape.

**21.** According to the poem, the pioneers compared the prairie to — **A** rotting roots … **B** the sea … **C** a little house … **D** sunflowers.

**22.** The poet describes prairie grass as if it were — **F** bear fur … **G** asters … **H** colorless … **J** extinct.

**23.** According to the poem, which is not characteristic of a prairie? **A** The wind blows on a prairie … **B** There are many tall trees on a prairie … **C** The plants and flowers on a prairie are fed by rotting roots … **D** Prairie soil is dark and fertile.

**24.** Which of the following statements is an opinion? **F** The little house was built on the prairie … **G** Goldenrod blooms on the prairie … **H** A prairie blown by the wind looks like a sea of grass … **J** Pioneers crossed the prairies.

# Unit 12: Comprehensive Test

## Practice Test 4: Listening, pp. 117–118

(Before you begin, be sure your child is using the bubble-in form on page 128 to record answers. Give your child scratch paper to take notes if needed.)

In this test you will use your reading skills to answer questions. This test is divided into two parts. For each part there is a sample exercise. Look at Sample A. I will read a sentence and the four answer choices. You will find the word that best completes the sentence. Listen carefully.

The man was very **hostile** to the people around him. To be **hostile** is to be — **A** foreign ... **B** quiet ... **C** helpful ... **D** unfriendly. Darken the circle for the word that best completes the sentence.

You should have darkened the circle for D, unfriendly, because a person who is hostile is "unfriendly."

Now you will do numbers 1 through 17. Listen carefully to the sentence and the four answer choices. Then darken the circle for the correct answer.

1. Olivia **frets** whenever she has to take a test. A person who frets — **A** worries ... **B** travels ... **C** swims ... **D** writes.
2. Her **arrogant** manner left her with few friends. To be arrogant is to be — **F** cheerful ... **G** conceited ... **H** talented ... **J** lonely.
3. They were told to bring a water **flask** on their camping trip. A flask is a kind of — **A** rope ... **B** bottle ... **C** barrel ... **D** bag.
4. They needed a **robust** person for a very physical job. *Robust* means — **F** weak ... **G** ill ... **H** strong ... **J** intelligent.
5. Why do these people have to **toil** so many hours for so little pay? *To toil* means to — **A** work ... **B** roam ... **C** write ...**D** journey.
6. Although the burglar was arrested, his **accomplice** was still at large. An accomplice is a — **F** hostage ... **G** relative ... **H** prisoner ... **J** partner.
7. Sean acted as the **sentry,** ready to let us know who was coming. A sentry is — **A** a guard ... **B** a servant ... **C** an athlete ... **D** a clerk.
8. They were **prohibited** from entering the vacant building. *Prohibited* means — **F** forgiven ... **G** encouraged ... **H** forbidden ... **J** taxed.
9. Playing cards was a good **diversion** for her while she waited to take some medical tests. A diversion is — **A** a distraction ... **B** an order ... **C** an assignment ... **D** a cure.
10. Washing one's hands is one way of preventing the spread of **contagious** diseases. Something that is contagious is — **F** contained ... **G** infectious ... **H** rare ... **J** common.
11. The **bizarre** situations the author described made her story unbelievable. *Bizarre* means — **A** normal ... **B** dreary ... **C** outlandish ... **D** detailed.
12. Do you know that your decision is **irrevocable?** Something that is irrevocable is — **F** reversible ... **G** unchangeable ... **H** important ... **J** simple.
13. The beautifully painted rooms **enhanced** the value of the house. *Enhanced* means — **A** heightened ... **B** decreased ... **C** simplified ... **D** diminished.
14. Cooking their own food helped them have an **economical** vacation. To be economical is to be — **F** expensive ... **G** enjoyable ... **H** thrifty ... **J** healthy.
15. Everyone wanted to stay indoors during this **dismal** weather. *Dismal* means — **A** bright ... **B** gloomy ... **C** windy ... **D** changeable.
16. The story's main character will **elude** his enemies and become a hero. *Elude* means — **F** escape from ... **G** cooperate with ... **H** work for ... **J** collide with.
17. Marla's little brother enjoyed the **saga** of King Arthur and his knights. A saga is a kind of — **A** journey ... **B** reward ... **C** toy ... **D** story.

Now turn to page 118.

Look at Sample B. I will read a passage and then ask a question. You will choose the best answer to the question. Listen carefully.

> Did you know that whales are not really fish? They look like fish, and they live in the water. But they are not fish. They are mammals, just like dogs and people. Some whales live in the tropics all year round, while others live in the Arctic. Still others migrate between the two regions every year.

Where do whales live? **A** only in the tropics ... **B** only in the Arctic ... **C** in both the tropics and the Arctic ... **D** in neither the tropics nor the Arctic. Darken the circle for the correct answer.

You should have darkened the circle for C, in both the tropics and the Arctic, because the passage states that whales live in both the tropics and the Arctic.

Find number 18. Listen carefully to the passage and the question. Then darken the circle for the correct answer. You will answer three questions.

> Thomas Edison was born in 1847 into a middle-class family. As a child,he caught a disease known as scarlet fever,which harmed his hearing. Edison is famous for the invention of the electric light. His work on an electric generator brought lighting into many American homes. Edison also made improvements to the telephone and telegraph. His greatest success may be the development of a modern research laboratory. Here,Edison made sound recordings and many other products. Edison received the exclusive rights to manufacture many of his devices. Foreign countries granted many of these rights.

**18.** As a child, Thomas Edison — **F** caught scarlet fever ... **G** invented the electric light ... **H** made improvements to the telephone ... **J** developed a research laboratory.

**19.** What did Edison do in his research laboratory? **A** invent the telegraph ... **B** worked on the electric generator ... **C** made sound recordings ... **D** found a cure for scarlet fever.

**20.** Thomas Edison was born in — **F** 1847 into a wealthy family ... **G** 1847 into a poor family ... **H** 1847 into an immigrant family ... **J** 1847 into a middle-class family.

Now find number 21. Listen to the information in this paragraph. You will answer three questions.

> We have probably all wondered just how much pollution we have been exposed to in our lifetime. According to an anatomy professor at Bergen University in Norway, it is possible to tell this by studying a person's teeth. The professor claims that teeth contain more information about a person's exposure to pollutants than blood or tissues. This professor accepts donations of teeth from people all over the world. When he receives a tooth, he grinds it down into a fine powder, which he tests for metals such as mercury, zinc, lead, and copper. The quantity and types of metals found in the tooth powder indicate the pollution a person has been exposed to. The professor uses his findings to draw conclusions about pollution in different parts of the world.

**21.** This selection would most likely be found in — **A** an almanac ... **B** a sports magazine ... **C** a science or health book ... **D** a fantasy book.

**22.** The author's purpose is to — **F** persuade people to send their teeth to a professor in Norway ... **G** present information ... **H** alarm people about pollution ... **J** warn people not to throw away their baby teeth.

**23.** What does the professor do with the information he gathers from teeth? **A** He sends it to environmental agencies ... **B** He draws conclusions about pollution in different areas ... **C** He writes a treatment plan for people who are ill ... **D** He predicts illnesses people are likely to get.

Now look at number 24. Listen to the story. You will answer three questions.

Jonathan wanted to meet new people,so he decided to audition for the school play. After speaking to the director,he found out when auditions were taking place. Jonathan ended up getting a minor role in the play,which meant he was only in one scene. The principal told the actors that they must keep their grades up to be in the play. Jonathan was very busy because he had to rehearse three times a week. Since Jonathan had such a great time being in the play, he marked his calendar for the next audition.

**24.** Why did Jonathan decide to audition for the school play? **F** he wanted to become famous ... **G** he wanted to meet new people ... **H** he was bored ... **J** the principal told him to.

**25.** How did he find out when auditions were taking place? **A** speaking to the director ... **B** talking to the principal ... **C** asking other actors ... **D** on the school calendar.

**26.** Jonathan marked his calendar for the next audition — **F** because the director asked him to ... **G** he wanted to stay busy ... **H** he had a great time being in the play ... **J** so he could keep his grades up.

Now find number 27. Listen to this announcement. You will answer two questions.

The local high school is announcing a concert festival for all seventh and eighth graders. To take part in the festival, you need to be a member of the band or orchestra. You can participate as a solo act or as part of a duo or trio. Band and orchestra teachers from other schools will serve as judges. If you're interested, complete the entry blank and include a check for five dollars.

**27.** Who is sponsoring the concert festival? **A** the local high school ... **B** the band and orchestra teachers ... **C** the PTA ... **D** the seventh-and eighth-grade bands and orchestras.

**28.** Participation in the concert festival is open to — **F** all seventh graders ... **G** all eighth graders ... **H** seventh-and eighth-grade band and orchestra members ... **J** only eighth-grade band members.

# Core Skills: Test Preparation

## INTRODUCTION

Standardized tests are becoming increasingly more important in both public and private schools, yet test anxiety causes many children to perform below their fullest potential. *Core Skills: Test Preparation* is designed to help children succeed on standardized tests. This program refreshes basic skills, familiarizes children with test formats and directions, and teaches test-taking strategies.

A large part of being well prepared for a test is knowing how to approach different types of questions and learning how to use time wisely. *Core Skills: Test Preparation* gives children the opportunity to take a test under conditions that parallel those they will face when taking standardized tests. This practice and experience will allow them to feel more confident when taking standardized tests and will enable them to demonstrate their knowledge successfully.

### Tools for Success

*Core Skills: Test Preparation* gives children valuable practice with the content areas and question formats of the major standardized tests used nationally.

*Core Skills: Test Preparation* provides the following:

- Test-taking strategies
- Familiarity with test directions
- Review of skills and content
- Awareness of test formats
- Practice tests

### Organization

The book is divided into units that correspond to those found on standardized tests.

- Reading Comprehension
- Reading Vocabulary
- Mathematics Problem Solving
- Mathematics Procedures
- Listening
- Language

*Core Skills: Test Preparation* is designed to ensure success on test day by offering the following:

**Strategies for Taking Reading Tests**
Unit 1 provides valuable test-taking strategies that help children do their best on the reading portion of any standardized test.

**Targeted Reading Objectives**
Unit 2 focuses on six reading objectives. Each practice question includes a hint to help your child master the targeted objective.

**Strategies for Solving Math Problems**
Unit 5 offers a step-by-step approach to solving word problems.

**Skill Lessons**
Units 3, 4, 6, 7, and 8 prepare your child by providing both content review and test-taking strategies. Each skill lesson includes the following:

*Directions*—state test instructions clearly, concisely, and in a format similar to that of standarized tests

*Try This*—offers a test strategy that helps children approach each question in a logical way

A *Sample*—familiarizes children with the "look and feel" of test items

*Think It Through*—specifically explains the correct answer to the Sample question

A *Practice Section*—contains a set of practice items that are focused on a specific skill and modeled on items from standardized tests

A *Unit Test*—covers all the skills in the lessons

**Practice Tests**
Units 9–13 simulate the content and format your child will encounter when taking standarized tests in reading comprehension, vocabulary, math, listening, and language.

## Using This Book

***Try This* and *Think It Through***
The *Try This* and *Think It Through* features accompany the sample questions on the skill lesson pages. Before your child answers the sample question, read the *Try This* skill strategy aloud. Give your child time to answer the question, and then review the correct answer using the information in *Think It Through*.

**Answering the Questions**
*Answer Bubbles*—Show your child how to fill in the multiple choice bubble-in answers. Stress the importance of filling the answer bubble completely, pressing firmly with the pencil, and erasing any stray marks. On the skill lesson pages, the answer bubbles are next to the answer choices. For the six practice tests, your child will use the bubble-in *Answer Sheet for Students* on pages 127–128.

*Short Answer Questions*—Standardized tests also require children to write the answers to some questions. *Core Skills: Test Preparation* gives children practice answering this type of question. Students should answer short answer, or open-ended, questions on a separate sheet of paper.

**Scripts for Listening Tests**
The lessons and tests in Unit 7 (pages 82–85) and Unit 12 (pages 117–118) require that an adult read a scripted text while the child answers the questions. These scripts are collected in the section titled *Listening Scripts* on pages vi–xii. The pages are perforated so that you can remove them easily. This way, your child can mark the answers in the book while you read from the loose pages.

**Practice Tests**
The six practice tests, pages 98–125, simulate standardized tests, providing your child with valuable practice before test day. Like many standardized tests, these are timed. The following are the suggested times needed to administer each test:

| | |
|---|---|
| Reading Comprehension | 35 minutes |
| Reading Vocabulary | 20 minutes |
| Math Problem Solving | 50 minutes |
| Math Procedures | 15 minutes |
| Listening | 25 minutes |
| Language | 35 minutes |

**Answer Sheet for Students**
On pages 127–128, you will find a bubble-in answer sheet very similar to the type of form your child will use during a standardized test. Your child will use this blank form to answer the six practice tests. If you think your child might want to repeat a test, be sure to copy the blank form *before* your child uses it.

**Answer Key**
A complete answer key begins on page 129. The pages are perforated so that you can remove them easily and return the book to your child. Note that pages 131–132 are a bubble-in form with the correct answers already entered. Do not confuse these pages with the blank Answer Sheet for Students on pages 127–128.

## Icons

This book contains the following icons to help you and your child:

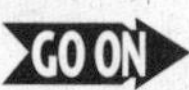

The **Go On** icon tells your child that the test continues on the next page.

The **Stop** icon tells your child to stop working.

The **Listen** icon tells you and your child that it is time to work together. Turn to the *Listening Scripts* section (pages vi–xii) to locate the script you need.

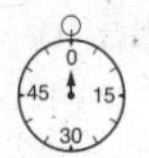

The stopwatch icon indicates the amount of time to allot for each **Practice Test**.

The lessons and practice tests in *Core Skills: Test Preparation* provide children with the tools they need to build self-confidence. That self-confidence can translate into a positive test-taking experience and higher scores on standardized tests. With its emphasis on skills, strategies for success, and practice, *Core Skills: Test Preparation* gives children the ability to succeed on standardized tests.

Name ______________________ Date ______________

# Unit 1: Reading Test-Taking Strategies

The following strategies will help you do your best on standardized reading tests. These three strategies will assist you in organizing the information needed to successfully answer the questions.

## STRATEGY 1
### The Check and See Strategy

This strategy can be used when a question asks for a fact from the passage. The answer to the question is right there in the passage. It is not hidden. Some of the same words may be in the passage and in the question.

 **Check and See** will help you answer *remembering information* questions.

**This is the Check and See Strategy**

1. **READ: Read** the question.
2. **FIND: Find** the words you need in the passage.
3. **DECIDE: Decide** which strategy to use.
   **Check and See:** Put a **check** next to the sentence where you can **see** the words you need to answer the question.
4. **ANSWER:** Choose the best **answer.**

GO ON

Name ______________________ Date ______________

## STRATEGY 2
### The Puzzle Piece Strategy

This strategy can be used when a question asks you what something means. Sometimes there does not seem to be an answer. It is not stated in the passage.

**Puzzle Piece** is the strategy to use when you must fit facts together to get the answer. This is like putting a puzzle together. Puzzles are made up of many pieces. You cannot look at one piece and know what the picture is. Only when you put the pieces together can you see the whole picture.

#### This is the Puzzle Piece Strategy

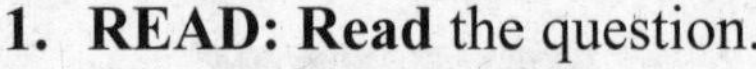

1. **READ: Read** the question.
2. **FIND: Find** the facts you need in the passage.
3. **DECIDE: Decide** which strategy to use.
   **Write: Write** the facts in puzzle pieces.
   **Put Together: Put** the puzzle pieces **together** to see the picture.
4. **ANSWER:** Choose the best **answer.**

GO ON

Name ________________________________ Date ________________

## STRATEGY 3
### The What Lights Up Strategy

This is another strategy you can use when an answer is not in the passage. To answer the question you need to add your own ideas to the passage. This added information can come from your own experiences.

**What Lights Up** can help you see if something is true, real, useful, or a fact. It can help you see what would happen if the story had a different ending.

You can use the **What Lights Up Strategy** to answer the hardest type of question. This is when you are asked to read and think of your own ideas. These questions are called *evaluating* and *extending meaning* questions.

#### This is the What Lights Up Strategy

1. **READ: Read** the question.
2. **FIND: Find** the facts you need in the passage.
3. **DECIDE: Decide** which strategy to use.
   **Write: Write** the facts in the book.
   **Think: Think** about your own ideas.
   **Light Up:** Think about what you have written.
   The answer will **light up** in your mind.
4. **ANSWER:** Choose the best **answer.**

STOP

Name ____________________ Date ____________

# Unit 2: Reading Comprehension

## SPECIFIC OBJECTIVES

**Objective 1:** **Determining word meanings**
Prefixes and suffixes, context clues, technical words, and words with multiple meanings

**Objective 2:** **Identifying supporting ideas**
Recalling facts and details, sequential order, following directions, and describing settings

**Objective 3:** **Summarizing main ideas**
Stated and implied main ideas, and identifying summaries

**Objective 4:** **Perceiving relationships and recognizing outcomes**
Cause-and-effect and making predictions

**Objective 5:** **Making inferences and generalizations**
Interpreting graphs and diagrams, inferring information, drawing conclusions, making judgments, and evaluating plot

**Objective 6:** **Recognizing points of view, facts, and opinions**
Author's purpose, persuasive language, and discerning facts and points of view

Name ______________________________ Date ______________

## OBJECTIVE 1: DETERMINING WORD MEANINGS

**Directions: Read each passage carefully. Darken the circle for the correct answer, or write your answer in the space provided.**

A word can have different meanings depending on when and how you use it. Readers can figure out the correct meaning of a word by reading the sentences around it.

Don was a base person. He kicked dogs and used bad language.

**1.** In this passage, base means —

Ⓐ moral.

Ⓑ heavy set.

Ⓒ solid.

Ⓓ having no decency.

*Hint: The second sentence explains the kind of person Don was.*

He made sure the base of the microscope was on a level surface. He didn't want anything sliding off.

**2.** In this passage, the word base means —

Ⓕ the bottom.

Ⓖ the essential ingredient.

Ⓗ a center of operations.

Ⓙ a substance that forms a salt.

*Hint: In this context, the base is part of the microscope.*

I was stopped by a police officer on April 1. Unfortunately, I was informed that my registration was invalid. The expiration date on it was March 31.

**3.** In this passage, the word invalid means —

Ⓐ too worn to read.

Ⓑ issued to the wrong person.

Ⓒ not valid.

Ⓓ sick.

*Hint: The explanation for* invalid *follows the use of the word.*

He had been in the nursing home only a short time, and he had to share a room with a much older man who was in very ill health. He complained to his daughter that he was not an invalid. He was a fully capable person.

**4.** In this passage, an invalid means —

Ⓕ a weak, sickly person.

Ⓖ a good roommate.

Ⓗ a good father.

Ⓙ someone who is not valid.

*Hint: Read the whole passage to get a sense of the word's meaning.*

GO ON

Name ______________________ Date ______________

## OBJECTIVE 1: DETERMINING WORD MEANINGS

Prefixes and suffixes are parts of some words. A prefix appears at the beginning of a word. A suffix appears at the end of a word. Both prefixes and suffixes affect the meaning of the word. Readers can use them to help figure out the meaning of a word.

John was a science fiction fan. He could not find enough to read about extraterrestrials.

**1.** In this passage, the word extraterrestrials means —

Ⓐ beings existing outside the earth's limits.

Ⓑ spaceships.

Ⓒ a type of terrapin.

Ⓓ the terrain on other planets.

*Hint: The prefix "extra-" means beyond, or out of.*

They had been to the amusement park before. Most of the rides were the same, but there was a fantastic new addition that the entire family could enjoy — a monorail!

**2.** In this paragraph, the word monorail means —

Ⓕ a type of mongoose.

Ⓖ a model railroad.

Ⓗ a single rail.

Ⓙ a one-man band.

*Hint: The prefix "mono-" means one.*

When he got rid of the computer, desk, easy chair, and bookcase, Joe's bedroom looked much more spacious.

**3.** What does the word spacious mean in this sentence?

______________________

______________________

______________________

______________________

______________________

______________________

______________________

______________________

*Hint: The suffix "-ious" means characterized by.*

GO ON

Name ______________________________ Date ______________

## OBJECTIVE 1: DETERMINING WORD MEANINGS

Sometimes you can figure out the meaning of a new or difficult word by using words around it as clues.

Garbage has always been a problem in big towns. In the 1700s, Benjamin Franklin had an idea for a municipal program in Philadelphia. He wanted to hire workers to dump garbage into the river.

1. In this paragraph, the word municipal means —
   - Ⓐ hungry.
   - Ⓑ country.
   - Ⓒ real.
   - Ⓓ city.

   *Hint: Read sentences 1 and 2.*

A trademark is the right a company has to own a brand name. No one else can use a trademark without the permission of the company that is the proprietor.

2. In this paragraph, the word proprietor means —
   - Ⓕ company name.
   - Ⓖ writer.
   - Ⓗ owner.
   - Ⓙ same brand.

   *Hint: Replace the underlined word with each of the choices.*

One popular misconception is that the Romans used two-wheeled chariots in battle. Although they raced with these small horse-drawn vehicles, they never fought with them.

3. What does the word chariots mean in this paragraph?

   ______________________________

   ______________________________

   ______________________________

   ______________________________

   ______________________________

   ______________________________

   ______________________________

   ______________________________

   *Hint: The underlined word is described in the passage.*

GO ON

Name ____________________ Date ____________

## OBJECTIVE 1: DETERMINING WORD MEANINGS

Specialized or technical words are words used in specific subjects, such as science and social studies. Readers can use all the other information in the text to help determine the meaning of these words.

Mark Twain was bankrupt after buying a machine for printing. After he lost his money, he paid off his debts by lecturing. He hated to lecture.

**1.** In this paragraph, the word bankrupt means—

Ⓐ unable to work.

Ⓑ home.

Ⓒ unable to pay debts.

Ⓓ into business.

*Hint: Read the first two sentences.*

Some Native American tribes were nomads. They moved from place to place following the buffalo, which were their food supply.

**2.** In this paragraph, the word nomads means —

Ⓕ wanderers.

Ⓖ settlers.

Ⓗ voters.

Ⓙ builders.

*Hint: Find the choice that describes people who move from place to place.*

Many people believe that Rome is the oldest metropolis still in existence. But other cities are much older. Rome was founded in 753 B.C. Damascus, Syria, was founded in 3000 B.C.

**3.** How is the word metropolis used in this paragraph?

______________________________

______________________________

______________________________

______________________________

______________________________

______________________________

______________________________

______________________________

*Hint: Think about what the paragraph is all about. What is the main idea?*

STOP

Name ______________________________ Date ______________

## OBJECTIVE 2: IDENTIFYING SUPPORTING IDEAS

Some facts or details are important. By noticing and remembering them, you will better understand what the passage is about.

When he was a child, Ray Ewry became ill with a fever. His doctors told him that he had polio. Polio is a disease that causes people to become paralyzed. Ray gradually got better, but he found that his legs had been weakened by his illness. The doctors thought that leg exercises might help him regain his strength. But they told Ray that he probably would never be able to walk and run as he once had.

For the next few years, Ray exercised daily. He did everything his doctors had recommended and more. After a while he could tell that his hard work was paying off. His legs became stronger and stronger. He even began to take part in track and field events.

**1.** The disease that Ray Ewry had was —

Ⓐ the measles.

Ⓑ chicken pox.

Ⓒ polio.

Ⓓ tuberculosis.

*Hint: Read the paragraph that talks about the disease.*

**2.** When he got better, Ray found that his legs were —

Ⓕ stronger.

Ⓖ weaker.

Ⓗ longer than before he got sick.

Ⓙ broken.

*Hint: Read the section about Ray getting better.*

**3.** For the next few years, Ray exercised —

Ⓐ every two weeks.

Ⓑ once a month.

Ⓒ weekly.

Ⓓ daily.

*Hint: Look for the sentence that starts with the same words.*

**4.** How did Ray overcome his disease?

______________________________

______________________________

______________________________

______________________________

______________________________

______________________________

______________________________

______________________________

*Hint: Read the last paragraph.*

GO ON

Soon Ray could jump higher and farther than most people. So he entered the Olympics in 1900 and signed up for three contests. He entered the standing high jump; the standing long jump; and the standing hop, step, and jump. He won gold medals, or first place, in all three events.

Ray repeated his amazing feat in 1904 and planned to try again in 1906. But before the next games, the hop, step, and jump was dropped from the list of events. So Ray had to settle for only two gold medals in 1906 and two again in 1908. Ray had indeed overcome his illness. In 1908, he held the record for the most Olympic gold medals ever given to any one person.

**5.** In the 1900 Olympics, Ray entered —

Ⓐ two events.

Ⓑ three events.

Ⓒ one event.

Ⓓ four events.

*Hint: Find the section that describes the events Ray entered in 1900.*

**6.** In 1900, Ray won gold medals in —

Ⓕ one event.

Ⓖ two events.

Ⓗ three events.

Ⓙ four events.

*Hint: Read the section about the 1900 Olympics.*

**7.** Ray held the record for the most —

Ⓐ jumps.

Ⓑ events.

Ⓒ gold medals.

Ⓓ Olympics.

*Hint: Read the last sentence in the second paragraph.*

**8.** Why was Ray unable to win the same gold medals in 1906 that he had won in 1904?

______

______

______

______

______

______

______

______

*Hint: Read how the games changed in 1906.*

GO ON

Name ______________________________ Date ______________

## OBJECTIVE 2: IDENTIFYING SUPPORTING IDEAS

Sometimes it is helpful to arrange events in the order they happened. This may help you to understand the passage better.

Boomerangs are one of the world's oldest weapons. They have been around for thousands of years. Scientists claim to have found a boomerang more than 2,400 years old, which makes the boomerang older than the bow and arrow.

The boomerang is usually thought of in connection with Australia, but it was used for hunting in Asia, Europe, and Africa, too. It was the Australian Aborigines, however, who designed boomerangs that returned after being thrown.

James Cook was the first explorer to see the Australian boomerang. In 1770, he described the strange flying sticks. The name probably came from a word that meant "wind." No one knows how the returning boomerang was invented. But scientists guess that a hunter accidentally made a curved throwing stick that came back.

Boomerangs are curved like a plane's wings on the top. They are flat on the bottom. This design helps them lift in the wind. Scientist T. L. Mitchell was the first person to explain why a boomerang returns. He wrote a paper about it in 1842.

**1.** When did James Cook first see boomerangs?

Ⓐ when he went hunting

Ⓑ before Mitchell studied boomerangs

Ⓒ thousands of years ago

Ⓓ when he went to Asia

*Hint: Compare each of the choices to when James Cook saw boomerangs.*

**2.** When were boomerangs invented?

Ⓕ before James Cook traveled to Australia

Ⓖ millions of years ago

Ⓗ after the bow and arrow

Ⓙ in 1842

*Hint: Compare each of the choices to the invention of the boomerang.*

**3.** What happened first?

Ⓐ Captain Cook saw boomerangs.

Ⓑ The Australian Aborigines used boomerangs.

Ⓒ T.L. Mitchell wrote a paper on boomerangs.

Ⓓ The bow and arrow was invented.

*Hint: You need to read all four paragraphs.*

**4.** Why are boomerangs able to lift in the wind?

______________________________

______________________________

______________________________

______________________________

______________________________

______________________________

______________________________

______________________________

*Hint: Read the last paragraph.*

GO ON

Name ______________________________ Date ______________

## OBJECTIVE 2: IDENTIFYING SUPPORTING IDEAS

Written instructions tell the reader how to do something. To follow them means to do them in the same order in which they were written.

Eric had to be especially careful cleaning the gutters because he was the one on the ladder and his friend was there only to hold the ladder. Eric carried a hose and a gardening tool up the ladder with him. The tool had a long handle, with it he was able to reach up and remove the leaves from the gutter above him. Once all the leaves were out, Eric ran the hose into the gutter to make sure it was running freely. He also sprayed the roof. Then he descended to the ground.

**1.** Eric ran the hose in the gutter —

Ⓐ before his friend held the ladder.

Ⓑ after he cleaned out the gutter.

Ⓒ after he sprayed the roof.

Ⓓ after he climbed down the ladder.

*Hint: Write down the sequence of events.*

**2.** According to the passage, what was the first thing Eric did?

Ⓕ carry the hose up the ladder

Ⓖ clean out the gutters

Ⓗ have his friend hold the ladder

Ⓙ treated his friend to breakfast as a way of saying thanks

*Hint: Usually, the first step is mentioned at the start.*

The model looked simple enough to assemble. Referring to the instructions, Nick first made sure that he had all the pieces required. He glued the chassis together, affixing the decals as he went along. The wheels simply snapped into place. After putting the batteries into both the remote and the car, he was ready to take it for a test drive.

**3.** Nick put the wheels on —

Ⓐ before referring to the instructions.

Ⓑ before inserting the batteries.

Ⓒ before gluing the chassis together.

Ⓓ before gathering all necessary pieces.

*Hint: Read the entire paragraph.*

**4.** What did Nick do before he began assembling the model?

______________________________

______________________________

______________________________

______________________________

______________________________

______________________________

______________________________

______________________________

*Hint: Read the beginning of the paragraph.*

STOP

Name ____________________ Date ____________________

# OBJECTIVE 3: SUMMARIZING MAIN IDEAS

The main idea is the overall meaning of a piece of writing. Often the main idea is written in the passage.

The harmless hognose snake is a champion bluffer. When this snake is threatened, it hisses and acts as if it will bite. If you don't run away, the hognose snake plays dead. It rolls over on its back, wiggling around as if it's in distress. Then it "dies" with its mouth open and tongue hanging out. If you turn it on its stomach, the snake will roll over on its back again.

**1.** The passage mainly tells —

- Ⓐ where the hognose snake is found.
- Ⓑ what things frighten the hognose snake.
- Ⓒ how dangerous the hognose snake is.
- Ⓓ how the hognose snake bluffs.

*Hint: The main idea is mentioned at the beginning of the passage.*

Doctors think that wearing red-tinted glasses can relieve sadness. Some people get very moody and sad in the winter. They may be affected by the short days. Bright lights can help some people, but not everyone. The reddish light coming through rose-colored glasses seems to make people feel happy.

**2.** What is the main idea of this selection?

- Ⓕ why happy people wear rose-colored glasses
- Ⓖ why some people get sad
- Ⓗ how short the daylight is in winter
- Ⓙ how colored glasses may help people feel better

*Hint: Again, the main idea is mentioned at the beginning.*

The Marines had a problem in World War II. Orders were sent in code, but the enemy kept learning the code. Nothing could be kept secret. Then someone thought that Navajo soldiers could help the Marines. Since very few other people could speak Navajo, this language was used as a code. No one on the enemy side knew Navajo, so the messages remained a secret.

**3.** What does this passage mainly talk about?

______________________________

______________________________

______________________________

______________________________

______________________________

______________________________

______________________________

______________________________

*Hint: The main idea is mentioned in the passage.*

GO ON

Name ____________________ Date ____________

## OBJECTIVE 3: SUMMARIZING MAIN IDEAS

Often the main idea is not given in the text. Sometimes the reader needs to figure it out by putting the facts together.

It takes more than food for babies to grow up healthy and happy. If babies are not patted and hugged, they grow more slowly and are less healthy. Also, they will not be as smart or happy as adults who were showered with affection when they were young.

**1.** The main idea of the passage is —

Ⓐ why good food is important to babies.

Ⓑ what makes babies grow up.

Ⓒ that children need love to grow up healthy and happy.

Ⓓ how to have smart children.

*Hint: What is the passage suggesting?*

One of the best-known rodeo cowboys in the world is Larry Mahan. Mahan was the national champion six times before he was thirty. He was good at every event. He was so successful that he had his own plane. When he got too old to ride, he started a rodeo school.

**2.** The passage mainly tells —

Ⓕ where to ride bulls and rope calves.

Ⓖ about the most famous rodeo cowboy in the world.

Ⓗ how to get rich in the rodeo.

Ⓙ where to go to rodeo school.

*Hint: You need to read the entire paragraph.*

Dogs have been called our best friends, but they are also good helpers. They can be used in many ways. Some dogs hunt, while others guard animals and property. Boxers and German shepherds can be trained to lead blind people. Doctors test some medicine on dogs. A dog named Laika was the first animal in space.

**3.** What is the main idea implied in the passage?

______________________________

______________________________

______________________________

______________________________

______________________________

______________________________

______________________________

______________________________

*Hint: The passage talks about dogs in general.*

GO ON

Name ____________________ Date ____________

## OBJECTIVE 3: SUMMARIZING MAIN IDEAS

A good summary contains the main idea of a passage. A good summary is brief, yet it covers the main points.

Dennis Chavez served in the United States Senate for more than twenty years. He was the first Hispanic to hold the post of senator. He was born in an adobe house in New Mexico. As a boy, he learned to speak English and taught it to his family. In 1920, he graduated from law school. Fifteen years later, he was elected senator from New Mexico. In 1991, a postage stamp with his picture was issued. The stamp honors his service to the country.

**1.** What is the best summary of this passage?

Ⓐ Dennis Chavez was elected senator in 1935.

Ⓑ Dennis Chavez was the first Hispanic United States senator.

Ⓒ Dennis Chavez taught his family to speak English.

Ⓓ Dennis Chavez worked at the post office.

*Hint: Look for the statement that sums up the passage.*

Many people take aspirin for aches and pains. Aspirin was first sold around 1900 by the Bayer Company of Germany. It was sold under the trademark "Aspirin." Then World War I swept across the world, and Germany lost the war. Under its terms of surrender, Germany agreed to release the trademark. The name Aspirin could no longer be used to sell only Bayer's product. It became the common name of a drug that can get rid of pain.

**2.** Write a brief summary of this passage.

____________________

____________________

____________________

____________________

____________________

____________________

____________________

____________________

*Hint: Be sure to include the main idea of the passage.*

GO ON

Name ______________________ Date ______________

Most slaves did not become famous, but Aesop was unusual. He was a clever, witty Greek slave who earned his freedom through his cleverness. He used his animal fables for the purpose of teaching people to respect the rights of others. Two thousand years later, people continue to use his stories to teach lessons or gain helpful advice.

**3.** Which of the following is the best summary of this passage?

Ⓕ Some Greeks were slaves.

Ⓖ Aesop's fables are still used to teach important lessons.

Ⓗ People have finally learned to respect others.

Ⓙ Many slaves became famous after they were freed.

*Hint: Look for the statement that sums up the passage.*

The akita is a Japanese hunting dog with short, bristly hair. It is considered a symbol of good health. In fact, the dog is so prized that it has been made an official national treasure of Japan. The first akita was brought into this country in 1937. Its owner was Helen Keller, the blind and deaf author.

**4.** What is this passage mostly about?

Ⓐ Japan's national treasures

Ⓑ Akitas were brought to the United States in 1937.

Ⓒ the fame of the akitas

Ⓓ Akitas are very popular in the United States.

*Hint: Which choice best describes the passage as a whole?*

*Acrophobia* means "fear of heights." People who have this fear are known as *acrophobics*. They aren't any less afraid even when there are fences or railings to protect them. Their fear is not just one of falling. Acrophobics may fear the desire to jump from any height.

**5.** Write a brief summary of this passage.

______________________________

______________________________

______________________________

______________________________

______________________________

______________________________

______________________________

______________________________

*Hint: Write about the main point of the passage.*

STOP

Name ______________________ Date ______________

# OBJECTIVE 4: PERCEIVING RELATIONSHIPS AND RECOGNIZING OUTCOMES

Often when we read, we need to see cause-and-effect relationships. Knowing what happened and what made it happen will help us to better understand what we read.

You may have seen movies in which the Roman emperor shows that a gladiator should die by turning down his thumb. Actually, the gory Roman custom was to turn a thumb up toward the heart to indicate death. A thumb down meant that the soldier should be allowed to live.

**1.** You can tell from the passage that death probably occurred —

Ⓐ once out of every five times.

Ⓑ when the emperor gave a thumbs up.

Ⓒ when the emperor gave a thumbs down.

Ⓓ only in the movies and not in real-life Rome.

*Hint: Death is the effect. What is the cause?*

In New York's Federal Reserve Bank, workers handle money and other valuable metals. One of the heaviest things workers must carry is a gold brick. For this reason, some of them wear special shoes made of magnesium. These shoes protect workers' toes if a brick falls on them.

**2.** Workers wear special shoes because —

Ⓕ they handle money.

Ⓖ they work in a bank.

Ⓗ they carry a gold brick.

Ⓙ they have special toes.

*Hint: The special shoes are the effect. Why are they worn?*

The anableps is a freshwater fish found in Mexico and parts of South America. It is unusual because of its eyes. A band of skin divides each eye in half, giving it four eyes. It stays near the top of the water. It can look above and below the water at the same time.

**3.** What is the best reason for why the anableps might have four eyes?

Ⓐ so it can live in Mexico

Ⓑ so it can see better than other fish

Ⓒ so it can live near the top of the water

Ⓓ There is no reason.

*Hint: The four eyes are the cause. What happens as a result of having them?*

Today's typewriter keyboard was first designed to slow down the speed of typing. The first typists typed too fast. This made the typewriters jam. The keys were arranged as they are today in order to force typists to slow down.

**4.** According to the passage, what made typists slow down?

______________________________

______________________________

______________________________

______________________________

*Hint: Slowing down is the effect. What made this happen?*

GO ON

Name ____________________ Date ____________

## OBJECTIVE 4: PERCEIVING RELATIONSHIPS AND RECOGNIZING OUTCOMES

Often the reader can predict or tell in advance, what is probably going to happen next. The reader must think about what would make sense if the story were to continue.

Kay threw her bike down wherever she stopped. More than once, she had left her bicycle in the driveway. Several times her dad had pointed out what could happen when she did this. One morning, as her dad was leaving for work, Kay heard a crashing sound outside.

**1.** What will Kay probably do next?

Ⓐ walk to school

Ⓑ buy a new bicycle

Ⓒ run outside

Ⓓ put her bicycle away

*Hint: Based on the other sentences, what seems most likely to happen next?*

Charlotte admired her mother's pearl ring. One morning, she decided she would wear it without her mother's permission. She dropped it in her purse and decided she would put it on at school. Later, she remembered the ring. When she reached into her purse, it was not there.

**2.** What is Charlotte likely to do next?

Ⓕ go through the contents of her purse more carefully

Ⓖ dump her purse out in the hall

Ⓗ call her mother

Ⓙ go to her next class

*Hint: Think about what you might do if you were Charlotte.*

Mary worked as a cook in a cafe. One day she got the great idea to cook the world's largest pancake. For days she worked to build a giant frying pan. Then, she mixed pancake batter all night long. Next, she poured the batter into the pan and heard the familiar sizzle.

**3.** What might happen next?

Ⓐ Mary will go to work in the cafe.

Ⓑ Mary will become famous.

Ⓒ Mary will have to prove that her pancake is the world's largest.

Ⓓ The pancake will burn.

*Hint: Read the entire paragraph to determine what Mary is most likely to do.*

Polio was once one of the most dreaded diseases in the United States. But in 1955, Jonas E. Salk helped change that. His polio vaccine was given to thousands of schoolchildren in Pittsburgh, Pennsylvania. Not one of the children came down with a case of polio.

**4.** What do you think happened next?

______________________________

______________________________

______________________________

______________________________

*Hint: Think about who else might benefit from this vaccine.*

STOP

Name ________________________________ Date ________________

## OBJECTIVE 5: MAKING INFERENCES AND GENERALIZATIONS

Often texts come with graphs or diagrams. These are there to help the reader better understand the passage.

**Brazil's Racial Mix in 1989**

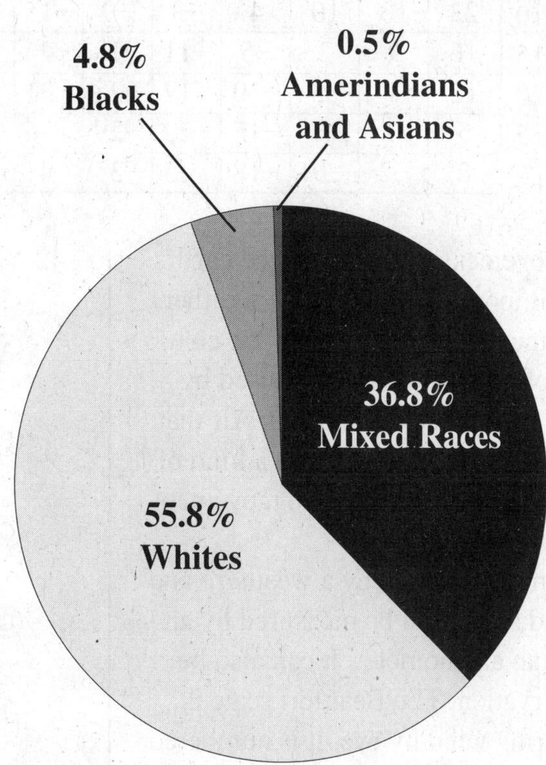


When the Portuguese arrived in Brazil early in the 16th century, it is estimated that there were between one and two million native Amerindian people. They were used as slaves, and many thousands died from diseases brought by the Europeans. Upon arrival in Brazil, the Portuguese settlers developed vast sugarcane estates, and for 150 years these estates were the world's main source of sugar. To work the estates, the owners used slaves from Africa. During Brazil's 400 years of Portuguese rule, marriages between Europeans and Indians, and Europeans and Africans, produced two new groups: the olive-skinned mestiços and the darker mulattos.

1. Which was the largest ethnic group in Brazil in 1989?
   - Ⓐ Amerindians
   - Ⓑ Portuguese
   - Ⓒ whites
   - Ⓓ those of mixed races

   *Hint: Look at the graph.*

2. How did the arrival of the Portuguese change Brazil's population?

   ________________________________________

   ________________________________________

   ________________________________________

   *Hint: Read the passage and review the chart.*

GO ON

Name ______________________ Date ______________

# WIND-CHILL FACTORS — EQUIVALENT TEMPERATURES

| Wind Speed (mph) | Air Temperature (°F) | | | | | | | | |
|---|---|---|---|---|---|---|---|---|---|
| | 35 | 30 | 25 | 20 | 15 | 10 | 5 | 0 | −5 |
| 0 | 35 | 30 | 25 | 20 | 15 | 10 | 5 | 0 | −5 |
| 5 | 33 | 27 | 21 | 16 | 12 | 6 | 0 | −5 | −10 |
| 10 | 22 | 16 | 10 | 4 | −3 | −9 | −15 | −24 | −27 |
| 15 | 16 | 9 | 2 | −5 | −11 | −18 | −25 | −32 | −38 |
| 20 | 12 | 4 | −3 | −10 | −17 | −25 | −31 | −39 | −46 |
| 25 | 5 | 0 | −7 | −15 | −22 | −29 | −36 | −44 | −51 |
| 30 | 0 | −2 | −10 | −18 | −25 | −33 | −41 | −4 | −56 |

**SHADED AREA**
Danger from freezing of exposed flesh

Wind is the movement of air across the earth's surface. It has an important effect on the weather. For instance, when cold air meets warm air, clouds and precipitation often form. Wind is caused by the heating of the atmosphere by the sun. Air that is warmed by the sun rises. This creates a kind of vacuum that is filled by cooler air. The movement of the air is wind.

Wind direction is measured by a weather vane or windsock. Wind speed can be measured by an instrument called an anemometer. It can also be measured by observation. The Beaufort scale is used when measuring wind by eye. It is numbered from 1 to 12. Another kind of measurement, called the wind-chill factor, involves the relationship between wind speed and temperature. The wind-chill factor is an indication of how much colder the wind makes the air feel.

**3.** What makes you feel coldest?

Ⓕ a temperature of 5 degrees and a wind of 5 miles per hour

Ⓖ a temperature of 15 degrees and a wind of 15 miles per hour

Ⓗ a temperature of 10 degrees and a wind of 10 miles per hour

Ⓙ a temperature of 30 degrees and a wind of 30 miles per hour

*Hint: You need to read the chart to determine the answer.*

**4.** Why might it be important to know the wind-chill factor?

Ⓐ If the wind-chill factor is 35 degrees, you know there's no wind.

Ⓑ If the wind-chill factor is -25 degrees or below, you could get frostbite.

Ⓒ Knowing the wind-chill factor will help you measure wind speed.

Ⓓ If you know the wind-chill factor, you can predict the next day's weather.

*Hint: Compare the choices to the chart.*

GO ON

Name ______________________ Date ______________

# OBJECTIVE 5: MAKING INFERENCES AND GENERALIZATIONS

When a reader makes an inference, it means that the information in the passage has told the reader something indirectly.

Mosquitoes are a tremendous problem in the summer. Mosquitoes love the hot weather. Then they can fly around and bite as many people as they want. Mosquitoes can't beat their wings in cool weather. The temperature must be more than sixty degrees for mosquitoes to fly.

**1.** You may conclude after reading the passage that —

- Ⓐ mosquitoes die in cold weather.
- Ⓑ people are not bothered by mosquitoes.
- Ⓒ mosquitoes go south for the winter.
- Ⓓ cool weather means fewer mosquito bites.

*Hint: Although never stated, the passage implies something.*

When Jim Abbott was born, part of his right arm had not formed completely. He had only one working hand, but Jim made the most of his situation. In college, Jim became the star pitcher of the baseball team. He played so well that he was later signed by a professional team. Jim Abbott became a major league player.

**2.** What does this passage infer?

- Ⓕ Abbott overcame his disability.
- Ⓖ People were not impressed by Abbott's skill.
- Ⓗ In college, Abbott was lazy.
- Ⓙ Abbott always regretted his disability.

*Hint: Look for the choice that is not written in the passage, but implied.*

One day, as Janna was jogging, she spotted something in the grass, so she decided to investigate. It was a wallet full of money. Janna knew she could keep the money, and no one would ever find out. But Janna also knew that the person who lost the wallet probably needed the money. So, she took the wallet to the police.

**3.** What can you conclude about Janna's personality after reading this passage?

______________________________

______________________________

______________________________

______________________________

______________________________

______________________________

______________________________

______________________________

*Hint: Janna's actions in the story tell you something about her.*

GO ON

Name ______________________________ Date ______________

# OBJECTIVE 5: MAKING INFERENCES AND GENERALIZATIONS

Sometimes a reader needs to generalize. This means to come up with a general statement about something in the text.

In 1883, a California mailman named Jim Stacy found a stray dog that he named Dorsey. Dorsey accompanied Stacy on his mail route. But later, Stacy got sick. So he tied the mail along with a note to Dorsey's back and sent the dog out alone. Dorsey delivered the mail in this fashion until 1886.

**1.** From this paragraph, you can guess that —

Ⓐ Stacy was sick for a long time.

Ⓑ Dorsey would never leave Stacy's side.

Ⓒ the note told people what to feed Dorsey.

Ⓓ Dorsey received a medal from the post office.

*Hint: Generalize what might have happened.*

The parasol ant of South America gets its name from the way it carries a bit of leaf over its head. But native Brazilians call them doctor ants. They use the ants' strong jaws to clamp down on deep cuts and keep them closed. Once the jaws clamp, the Brazilians pinch off the ants' bodies to keep the wound sealed.

**2.** From the passage, you can make the general statement that —

Ⓕ parasol ants haven't been named correctly.

Ⓖ the ants' jaws stay closed after the ants die.

Ⓗ native Brazilians named the ants "parasol ants."

Ⓙ the ants like sunshine.

*Hint: Which choice is the best guess?*

Great Britain may not be the place where golf was first played. The ancient Romans played a similar game. They used a curved stick and a leather ball stuffed with feathers. The Romans occupied Great Britain until A.D. 400.

**3.** From this passage, you could make the generalization that golf —

Ⓐ began in A.D. 400.

Ⓑ began in Great Britain and moved to Rome.

Ⓒ began in Rome and moved to Great Britain.

Ⓓ is played more today in Rome than in Great Britain.

*Hint: Eliminate the choices that can be proved untrue.*

GO ON

Name ______________________________ Date ______________

# OBJECTIVE 5: MAKING INFERENCES AND GENERALIZATIONS

A good reader will analyze what he or she reads and make his or her own judgment about the text. Often things are implied in a text, rather than stated directly.

People around the world eat many different things. Some people eat worms and ants. In some areas of the world, termites are considered a healthy food. They make delicious, bite-sized snacks. They are even served with hamburgers.

1. What judgment can you make after reading this paragraph?

   Ⓐ Eating habits differ around the world.

   Ⓑ Hamburgers are made of ants and worms.

   Ⓒ Everyone in the world eats the same things.

   Ⓓ Termites are better than worms.

   *Hint: You need to read the entire paragraph. Think about the point that is being made.*

Do you like peanut butter? Most people do. Naturally, peanut butter is made from peanuts. But peanuts are used in the manufacture of other things. Items such as ink dyes, shaving cream, paper, and shoe polish use peanuts in some form.

2. The passage suggests that —

   Ⓕ peanut butter is a good shaving cream.

   Ⓖ shoe polish tastes like peanut butter.

   Ⓗ it is easy to write on a peanut.

   Ⓙ peanuts are very useful.

   *Hint: Review the facts. What do they say about peanuts?*

The giant saguaro cactus plant is often seen in American Western movies. Although the largest plants can grow to be forty feet tall, they grow very slowly at first. The stem of the plant grows about one inch during its first ten years, but later it grows at a faster rate. The largest saguaros can live for almost two hundred years.

3. Based on the information in the passage, the saguaro would most likely be found —

   Ⓐ in Japan.

   Ⓑ in New York.

   Ⓒ in the Middle East.

   Ⓓ in Arizona.

   *Hint: None of the choices are stated in the passage, but one of them is a conclusion that the reader can determine after reading the text.*

Elizabeth Tashjian runs the world's only nut museum. The museum is found on the first floor of an old mansion, which is also her home. Her collection of nuts from around the world is always being raided by bushy-tailed thieves that live near the house.

4. What were the bushy-tailed thieves that raided the museum?

   ______________________________

   ______________________________

   ______________________________

   ______________________________

   *Hint: The clues are in the passage.*

Name ______________________ Date ______________

# OBJECTIVE 5: MAKING INFERENCES AND GENERALIZATIONS

The setting is the when and where of a story. The characters are the people or people-like figures in the story. The plot is the sequence of events that make up the core of the story.

The organ starts, and its music fills the air. The horses slowly begin to move. Riders hold tightly as their colorful horses go up and down and around and around.

**1.** What is the setting of this passage?

_______________________________

_______________________________

_______________________________

_______________________________

*Hint: Picture the scene in your mind.*

In the 17th century, the Incas of South America had an empire that stretched more than 2,500 miles. They built highways throughout their empire. They built tunnels through mountain cliffs. One of their rope suspension bridges is still used today.

**2.** The Incas' Empire was in —

- Ⓐ the southern United States.
- Ⓑ South Africa.
- Ⓒ South America.
- Ⓓ a southern state.

*Hint: Read the first sentence.*

**3.** This passage describes a period of time in the —

- Ⓕ 1600s.
- Ⓖ 1700s.
- Ⓗ 1800s.
- Ⓙ 1900s.

*Hint: Read the first sentence.*

In Greek legends, Orpheus was a singer of sweet music. As a young man, he married a beautiful woman named Eurydice. But then she stepped on a poisonous snake and died. Orpheus was filled with grief, and he decided to go to the underworld to win his wife back from death. In the dark caverns below the earth, he charmed Hades, king of the underworld, with his sad song. Hades agreed to release Eurydice on one condition: Orpheus could not look back at her until they reached the earth's surface. Orpheus agreed, and he began to lead his wife from the darkness. But just once, to make sure she was still following, Orpheus looked back. His dear wife vanished instantly.

**4.** Which of the characters is very powerful?

- Ⓐ Orpheus
- Ⓑ Eurydice
- Ⓒ Hades
- Ⓓ none of the characters

*Hint: Think about what each character did.*

**5.** Describe the overall mood that the author establishes in this passage.

_______________________________

_______________________________

_______________________________

_______________________________

_______________________________

*Hint: Think about the words used to tell the story.*

STOP

Name ______________________________ Date ______________

# OBJECTIVE 6: RECOGNIZING POINTS OF VIEW, FACTS, AND OPINIONS

The author's point of view is what he or she feels about what he or she is writing. Opinions express points of view.

The island of Surtsey, off the southern coast of Iceland, was the first new island to appear in the North Atlantic in two hundred years. Scientists studied how plant life began on the island and how long the island may last. They determined whether the island would be destroyed by the same volcano that created it. Their research gave the public a wealth of information about this unusual island.

**1.** The author feels that the scientists' study of Surtsey —

Ⓐ made it famous.
Ⓑ made them wealthy.
Ⓒ was unnatural.
Ⓓ was a waste of their time.

*Hint: Read the entire paragraph.*

Would you like to come home after a long day and walk into an elephant? You would do that if you lived in The Elephant House in Margate, New Jersey, which was built in 1881 by James Lafferty. Herbert Green built a chicken-shaped house in 1962. Sarah Winchester spent 38 years building a ghost-proof house with fake chimneys, doors that opened into walls, and stairs that led nowhere. And a man named Baldasera spent forty years building an underground house with ninety rooms for about $300. If you think your plans for a house are too unusual, think again!

**2.** This author believes that —

Ⓕ no house plans are too unusual.
Ⓖ people should stick with traditional designs.
Ⓗ underground homes are impractical.
Ⓙ homes should be built quickly.

*Hint: Think about what the author says about homes.*

Bill Cosby had planned to be a teacher one day. But he dropped out of college and became a successful actor instead. In 1971, he decided to go back to school. He finished his degree and went to receive his doctor of education degree in 1977. As part of his coursework, he developed programs for *Sesame Street* and *The Electric Company.* He also worked with Captain Kangaroo to produce *Picture Page,* a television series for children.

**3.** The point of view this author expresses is that —

Ⓐ you should never give up on your dreams.
Ⓑ Cosby became successful because of children's programming.
Ⓒ Cosby would have been a better teacher than he was an actor.
Ⓓ it took Cosby too long to get his degree.

*Hint: Review each choice. With which one would the author most likely agree?*

The whole family once piled into the car and headed to the drive-in movies. Beneath the stars, we would munch popcorn and watch a movie. The first drive-in movie opened in New Jersey in 1933. Now there are only a few left.

**4.** What does the author think of drive-in movies?

______________________________

______________________________

______________________________

*Hint: What feeling do you get when you read this?*

GO ON

Name ______________________________ Date ______________

## OBJECTIVE 6: RECOGNIZING POINTS OF VIEW, FACTS, AND OPINIONS

Often authors want to convince their readers of something. To do this, they will only write about their own point of view. They use descriptive and emotional language that backs up their point of view.

How much is a seat in Congress worth: $5 million, $17 million, $30 million? In a recent California election, two millionaires were vying for the same Senate seat. Together they spent more than $30 million on their campaigns. The losing candidate spent more than $17 million in his bid to be senator. Isn't it time we stopped this extravagance? We need to develop laws that stop the buying of seats in Congress. Only by limiting the amount of money candidates may receive and use when running for office will we be able to reduce the extravagance that now exists in Congressional elections.

**1.** Which of the statements below is an opinion?

Ⓐ Millionaires are running for Congress.

Ⓑ Running for Congress has become an extravagance.

Ⓒ Having $17 million does not guarantee a seat in Congress.

Ⓓ A candidate is someone who runs for office

*Hint: An opinion is a point of view.*

**2.** What does the author of this editorial want U.S. citizens to do?

______________________________

______________________________

______________________________

______________________________

*Hint: Read the entire paragraph.*

The President has proposed that all young Americans be encouraged to participate in a national service plan. The theory is that this will instill a greater sense of community in this so-called "lost" generation. The younger generation is supposedly selfish, but the facts don't warrant these conclusions. Over 800 colleges have organized volunteer efforts, and most high schools have students doing community service. Troubled young adults are the exception, not the rule; the press reports the opposite in its effort to sell papers. In order to teach young people the skills and values necessary to become productive citizens, it would be far better to increase their numbers in the private sector.

**3.** Which statement best expresses the author's opinion about national service programs?

Ⓕ They are being introduced by the President.

Ⓖ They have benefited our country through the years.

Ⓗ They will rebuild the American Dream.

Ⓙ They are not as effective as the private sector in teaching values.

*Hint: Read the entire paragraph.*

**4.** Who does the author blame for creating the public opinion that young adults are selfish?

______________________________

______________________________

______________________________

*Hint: The answer is stated in the paragraph.*

GO ON

Name ______________________ Date ____________

## OBJECTIVE 6: RECOGNIZING POINTS OF VIEW, FACTS, AND OPINIONS

It is important to recognize the difference between fact and opinion. A fact is real and true. An opinion states a point of view. Descriptive words are used to offer opinions.

Most people are afraid of something. A study was conducted to determine what people fear most. The research found that men and women tend to have the same fears. The basic difference is the order in which they rate these fears. For example, men fear bats and speaking in public more than women do. Women fear fire, dead people, and rats more than men do.

**1.** It is a fact that —

Ⓐ men's and women's fears are somewhat alike and yet different.

Ⓑ everyone likes rats.

Ⓒ women fear bats more than men do.

Ⓓ everyone is afraid of chickens.

*Hint: Which choice best matches what is said in the passage?*

Some animals can help predict earthquakes. This was proven in China in 1974. Just a few months before a huge earthquake struck an area, animals began acting strange. Hens wouldn't roost, and geese wouldn't fly. Pigs tried climbing walls and fought with each other. Even hibernating snakes crawled out of the ground. The Chinese paid attention to these warnings. Many people left the area before the earthquake struck.

**2.** This passage states the fact that —

Ⓕ some animals know if an earthquake is going to occur.

Ⓖ many earthquakes occur in China.

Ⓗ the pigs were fighting with the chickens.

Ⓙ animals in China act strange all the time.

*Hint: You need to read the entire paragraph.*

Man o' War was a wonderful racehorse. He won 20 of 21 races and set five world records. When Man o' War died in 1947, his owner, Samuel Riddle, had him buried. Riddle, who died in 1963, remembered the horse in his will. He left $4 million to maintain Man o' War's grave, which the horse richly deserved.

**3.** Which of the following is a fact?

Ⓐ Man o' War was a wonderful racehorse.

Ⓑ Man o' War died in 1947.

Ⓒ Samuel Riddle was an eccentric person.

Ⓓ The horse deserved a $4 million inheritance.

*Hint: A fact is real and true.*

Sarah Winnemucca was a pioneer of Native American rights. Her father was a chief of the Paiute tribe in Nevada. As a child, she moved to California, where she lived with a white family. She learned to speak English. As an adult, she became a teacher and tried to make peace between the white settlers and her native tribe. She even met to discuss the situation with President Hayes. She gained the support of many people, and her efforts were valuable.

**4.** It is the writer's opinion that Winnemucca —

Ⓕ should not have moved to California.

Ⓖ was a good teacher.

Ⓗ liked President Hayes.

Ⓙ made worthwhile efforts.

*Hint: Look at the words that describe Winnemucca.*

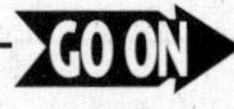

Name ____________________ Date ____________

# OBJECTIVE 6: RECOGNIZING POINTS OF VIEW, FACTS, AND OPINIONS

Sometimes the point of view will change during a story. A character can change how he or she feels and/or the mood of a story can change.

Bob had two left feet. He was so embarrassed, that he would never get up and dance. One day, he decided to do something about it, so he signed up for dance lessons. The dance instructor told him how to move his feet. It was supposed to be the box step; unfortunately, Bob tripped over his own feet.

After several lessons, Bob could do the box step smoothly and with confidence. He couldn't wait to get up and dance.

**1.** With which statement would the author of this passage most likely agree?

Ⓐ Some people should never try to dance.

Ⓑ Do not give up.

Ⓒ Lessons never help you to improve.

Ⓓ Some people are natural born dancers.

*Hint: Read the last paragraph.*

**2.** How did Bob change during the story?

______________________________

______________________________

______________________________

______________________________

______________________________

______________________________

______________________________

______________________________

*Hint: Read the first two and last two sentences.*

"I don't want to write a story about girls! I don't know anything about girls," Louisa May Alcott told her publisher, Mr. Niles. But she was desperate for money. So Louisa wrote a simple story about growing up with four sisters in a family that had no money. Her book, *Little Women,* took a year to write. Mr. Niles thought the book was dull, and so did Louisa, but in three months, all the copies of *Little Women* had sold. Mr. Niles thought he could sell three or four hundred more copies. With a great sigh of relief, Louisa was able to write to her family, "Paid off all the debts, thank the Lord! Now I feel that I could die in peace."

**3.** Louisa May Alcott did not want to write *Little Women* because —

Ⓕ the story was too exciting for most readers.

Ⓖ she hated children.

Ⓗ she felt she didn't know enough about girls.

Ⓙ Mr. Niles did not offer her enough money.

*Hint: Read the first sentence.*

**4.** Why was Louisa relieved after the book was published?

______________________________

______________________________

______________________________

*Hint: Read the last 5 sentences.*

STOP

Name ______________________________ Date ______________

# Unit 3: Reading Comprehension

## READING SELECTIONS

**Directions: Read the selection carefully. Darken the circle for the correct answer, or write your answer in the space provided.**

| **Try This** | Read each selection and each question twice. Check your answers by looking back in the selection. |
|---|---|

**Sample A** **Cliff Dwellings**

Mesa Verde National Park, in southwestern Colorado, has some of the best examples of ancient cliff dwellings in the United States. About 800 years ago, people called the Anasazi built apartment-like dwellings in the caves of steep canyon walls.

Where is Mesa Verde National Park?

Ⓐ New Mexico

Ⓑ Utah

Ⓒ Texas

Ⓓ Colorado

| **Think It Through** | The correct answer is D. The first sentence states that the park is in southwestern Colorado. |
|---|---|

STOP

### The Nomads of Kazakhstan

Nomads are people who move around from place to place during the year. Nomads usually move when the seasons change so that they will have enough food to eat. Herding, hunting, gathering, and fishing are all ways that different nomadic groups get their food.

Nomads that herd animals are called pastoral nomads. Their way of life depends on the seasonal movement of their herds. Pastoral nomads may herd cattle, horses, sheep, goats, yaks, reindeer, camels, or other animals. Instead of keeping their animals inside fenced pastures, pastoral nomads let them graze on open fields. However, they must make sure the animals do not overgraze and damage the pastureland. To do this, they keep their animals moving throughout the year. Some pastoral nomads live in steppe or desert environments. These nomads often have to move their animals very long distances between winter and summer pastures.

The Kazakhs of Central Asia are an example of a pastoral nomadic group. They have herded horses, sheep, goats, and cattle for hundreds of years. Because they move so much, the Kazakhs do not have permanent homes. They bring their homes with them when they travel to new places. The Kazakhs live in tent-like structures called yurts. Yurts are circular structures made of bent poles covered with thick felt. Yurts can be easily taken apart and moved. They are perfect homes for the Kazakhs' nomadic lifestyle.

During a year, a Kazakh family may move its herd of sheep, horses, and cattle as far as 500 miles (805 km). For one Kazakh family, each year is divided into four different parts. The family spends the first part of

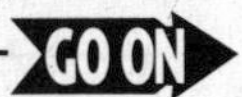

Name ______________________________ Date ______________

the year in winter grazing areas. Then, in early spring, they move to areas with fresh grass shoots. When these spring grasses are gone, the family moves their animals to summer pastures. In the fall, the animals are kept for six weeks in autumn pastures. Finally, the herds are taken back to their winter pastures. Each year, the cycle is repeated.

The nomadic lifestyle of the Kazakhs has changed, however. In the early 1800s, people from Russia and eastern Europe began to move into the region. These people were farmers. They started planting crops in areas that Kazakhs used for pasture. This made it more difficult for Kazakhs to move their animals during the year. Later, when Kazakhstan was part of the Soviet Union, government officials encouraged the Kazakhs to settle in villages and cities. Many Kazakhs still move their animals during the year, but tending crops is now another important way they get food.

**1.** Why does the author begin the selection by defining nomads?

Ⓐ The word *nomad* is not in the dictionary.

Ⓑ Not all readers may be familiar with nomads

Ⓒ Nonfiction almost always starts with a definition.

Ⓓ Definitions are always interesting to read.

**2.** What is the *main* purpose for this selection?

Ⓕ to persuade readers to preserve the Kazakh way of life

Ⓖ to describe the way of life of nomadic Kazakhs

Ⓗ to express his or her feelings about the nomadic way of life

Ⓙ to describe the impact of Russian immigrants on Kazakh nomads

**3.** The author says, "They are perfect homes for the Kazakhs' nomadic lifestyle." Why does the author use the word perfect?

Ⓐ The yurts the nomads live in are very high quality *yurts* with amazing features.

Ⓑ The word *yurt* means "perfect" in the language of the Kazakhs.

Ⓒ Even though the author is not necessarily a nomad, he or she probably lives in a yurt and likes it.

Ⓓ Even though living in a yurt might not appeal to everyone, the author thinks it works well for nomads.

**4.** What is the significance of the change in the Kazakh nomads' way of life?

Ⓕ The way of life may become lost forever.

Ⓖ The nomads are becoming more modern and urban.

Ⓗ The way of life will spread to other cultures and places.

Ⓙ The nomads will form their own nation.

**5.** Which statement supports the idea that the Kazakh nomads have been pressured to change their lifestyle?

Ⓐ Government officials encouraged the Kazakhs to settle in villages and cities.

Ⓑ Their way of life depends on the seasonal movement of their herds.

Ⓒ They must make sure the animals do not overgraze and damage the pastureland.

Ⓓ The nomadic lifestyle of the Kazaks has changed.

**6.** Based on the context of the third paragraph, the word *pastoral* means —

Ⓕ musical.

Ⓖ of the village.

Ⓗ of the country.

Ⓙ urban.

GO ON

Name ______________________________ Date ______________

7. A compound word is made from two words that are joined together. The compound word is related in meaning to the two original words. Which of the following words from the selection is a compound word?

   Ⓐ environments Ⓒ another
   Ⓑ overgraze Ⓓ nomads

8. Because the Kazakhastan move so much —

   Ⓕ they enjoy hunting.
   Ⓖ they do not have permanent homes.
   Ⓗ they have friends in many places.
   Ⓙ they do not have pets.

9. In the last paragraph, which sentence *best* summarizes the selection?

______________________________

______________________________

______________________________

## A Poison Tree

by William Blake

I was angry with my friend:
I told my wrath, my wrath did end.
I was angry with my foe;
I told it not, my wrath did grow.

And I water'd it in fears,
Night & morning with my tears;
And I sunned it with my smiles
And with soft deceitful wiles.[1]

And it grew both day and night,
Till it bore an apple bright;
And my foe beheld it shine,
And he knew that it was mine,

And into my garden stole
When the night had veil'd the pole[2]:
In the morning glad I see
My foe outstretch'd beneath the tree.

**1 wiles:** tricks **2 pole:** the North or South pole

14. What emotion does the apple *most likely* symbolize for the speaker?

______________________________

______________________________

______________________________

______________________________

11. In stanza 1, the speaker says, "I was angry with my foe; I told it not, my wrath did grow." What does the speaker mean?

   Ⓐ By not telling a friend about the speaker's anger at an enemy, the anger grows.
   Ⓑ After telling a friend that he is angry, the speaker's anger goes away.
   Ⓒ By not confessing his anger to his enemy, the speaker's anger gets stronger.
   Ⓓ After telling his enemy that he is angry, the speaker's anger goes away.

12. What is the effect of the use of first person in this selection?

   Ⓕ It makes the events more believable.
   Ⓖ It allows the author to use more persuasive language.
   Ⓗ It emphasizes the speaker's feelings.
   Ⓙ It helps the reader better understand the enemy's point of view.

13. What is the effect of rhyme throughout the poem?

   Ⓐ It creates a regular rhythm and emphasizes key words.
   Ⓑ It turns prose into poetry and makes it more meaningful.
   Ⓒ It differentiates between good and evil and softens the message.
   Ⓓ It allows more meaning naturally and in fewer words.

GO ON

Name ____________________________ Date ______________

## A Letter to the Editor of the Daily Tribune

Mr. Michael Cowling, Editor

Daily Tribune

Dear Mr. Cowling,

The Monroe Library has helped me a great deal in the last few months. I was having trouble reading. My teacher told us that the library has an after-school program. The people there could help kids with homework and reading. My mom signed me up. I go to the library right after school. Ms. Rose tutors me in reading for a half-hour every day. Then I do my homework.

My grades have improved. I have more time to practice and play baseball. Mom is happy because I finish my homework early. Sometimes I go back to the library in the evening for programs like cartoon workshops and storytelling.

The library also has a homework hotline. Students can call, and someone will try to answer their questions.

I never thought the library could be so much fun. I hope you will print this letter so more kids can learn about the library's great programs.

Sincerely,

Joshua Cohen

Joshua Cohen

GO ON

Name ______________________ Date ______________

**14.** Who is Michael Cowling?

Ⓕ the reading tutor at the Monroe Library

Ⓖ the author of this letter

Ⓗ the editor of the *Daily Tribune*

Ⓙ Joshua's teacher

**15.** When does Joshua go to the library?

Ⓐ on the weekends

Ⓑ after school

Ⓒ before school

Ⓓ during lunch

**16.** Who told Joshua about the after-school program?

Ⓕ his mother

Ⓖ his teacher

Ⓗ Ms. Rose

Ⓙ the librarian

**17.** This letter is written from the viewpoint of someone who is —

Ⓐ angry.

Ⓑ grateful.

Ⓒ confused.

Ⓓ upset.

**18.** Which of these is an *opinion* in the letter?

Ⓕ My grades have improved.

Ⓖ My teacher told us that the library has an after-school program.

Ⓗ I never thought the library could be so much fun.

Ⓙ Ms. Rose tutors me in reading for a half-hour every day.

**19.** From the letter you can conclude that Joshua —

Ⓐ will never go back to the library.

Ⓑ enjoys spending time at the library.

Ⓒ still has problems at school.

Ⓓ is not feeling well.

**20.** Why did Joshua go to the Monroe Library?

______________________________________

______________________________________

______________________________________

______________________________________

______________________________________

______________________________________

______________________________________

______________________________________

**21.** This letter is written in order to —

______________________________________

______________________________________

______________________________________

______________________________________

______________________________________

______________________________________

______________________________________

______________________________________

GO ON

Name ______________________________ Date ______________

## Niagara Falls Journal

**July 24**—My family and I got an early morning start on our driving vacation from Illinois to Niagara Falls in Ontario, Canada. We drove the entire 11 hours today. I am excited because this is the first time I have visited another country. I love reading the street signs and food labels in French and English. How unusual to be in a country that is *bilingual!*

**July 25**—We started our day at Horseshoe Falls. Just watching all the millions of gallons of water flow over the Falls is *mesmerizing.* I couldn't take my eyes off the natural display. The noise was incredible. Where does all that water come from? My family and I decided to take the tour of the tunnels that are under Horseshoe Falls. We had to wear raincoats and ride an elevator down to the tunnels. We walked through long tunnels that made me feel *claustrophobic* until we could see daylight and hear the roar of the rushing water. Unbelievable! We were seeing the waterfall from behind. I learned the following amazing facts about the Falls: Niagara Falls is made up of two falls, the Horseshoe Falls in Canada and the American Falls in the United States. Horseshoe Falls is 167 feet (51 meters) high and 2,600 feet (792 meters) wide. American Falls is 176 feet (54 meters) high and 1,000 feet (305 meters) wide.

**July 26**—Today we went on the *Maid of the Mist* boat ride. Again we had to put on raincoats, but this time they were much heavier than the ones we wore in the tunnels. We needed added protection because our boat took us past the American Falls and into the heavy mist of Horseshoe Falls. As we neared Horseshoe Falls, the noise sounded like a train coming closer and closer. It was hard to keep my balance standing in the boat, because the force of the water was so great. For a few seconds I was afraid that our boat would get swallowed by the whirlpool that the Falls create. I took some good pictures of the Falls and the rainbow produced by the mist and the sun. We came back to the Falls at night to see the light display. Hundreds of lights that constantly changed color were directed on the Falls.

**July 27**—We rented two tandem bicycles today. We rode the bike path along the Niagara River from Horseshoe Falls to Fort Erie. The ride was long, but the view of the rapidly moving Niagara River was gorgeous. Fort Erie was constructed by the British in 1764. It was used as a supply depot and a port for ships transporting merchandise, troops, and passengers from Lake Erie along the Niagara River to the upper Great Lakes. My favorite point of interest in the fort was the soldiers' barracks. You could see how cramped and unpleasant their daily life must have been.

**July 28**—We left Niagara Falls for the remainder of our trip to Toronto, Ontario. We drove along Queen Victoria Park, which parallels the Niagara River. I agree with Winston Churchill, who once remarked that this route is "the prettiest Sunday afternoon drive in the world."

GO ON

Name ______________________________ Date ______________

**22.** What is the author's mood in the first paragraph?

Ⓕ nervousness

Ⓖ boredom

Ⓗ irritation

Ⓙ enthusiasm

**23.** You can tell that the word *bilingual* means —

Ⓐ a number system based on 2.

Ⓑ having two languages.

Ⓒ wealthy.

Ⓓ a dry stream bed.

**24.** In the second journal entry, the phrase "made me feel claustrophobic" means the author was —

Ⓕ afraid of water.

Ⓖ willing to climb to great heights.

Ⓗ afraid of confined places.

Ⓙ used to traveling in boats.

**25.** Which is a *fact* expressed in the journal?

Ⓐ I love reading the street signs and food labels in French and English.

Ⓑ My favorite point of interest in the fort was the soldiers' barracks.

Ⓒ American Falls is higher than Horseshoe Falls.

Ⓓ The postcards sold at Niagara Falls are prettier than anywhere else on earth.

**26.** In the second journal entry, what word does the author use to mean "can't take my eyes off?"

Ⓕ mesmerizing

Ⓖ incredible

Ⓗ display

Ⓙ claustrophobic

**27.** In the third journal entry, the noise of Horseshoe Falls is compared to —

Ⓐ a boat.

Ⓑ noises in tunnels.

Ⓒ noise created by a whirlpool.

Ⓓ an approaching train.

**28.** Why was Fort Erie built?

Ⓕ as a supply depot and port

Ⓖ as a place for tourists to visit

Ⓗ as a lighthouse and store

Ⓙ as a place for the queen to live

**29.** The description of the soldiers' barracks at Fort Erie helps the reader know that —

Ⓐ the soldiers' families lived with them.

Ⓑ the soldiers were content at the fort.

Ⓒ the soldiers had many chores.

Ⓓ the soldiers were very uncomfortable.

**30.** What does the last journal entry describe?

______________________________

______________________________

______________________________

______________________________

**31.** What was the author's purpose in keeping this journal?

______________________________

______________________________

______________________________

______________________________

______________________________

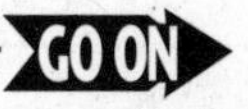

Name ____________________ Date ____________

*NEW AND IMPROVED*

# Grade A Dog Chow

**A new and improved line of dog food that combines the flavor of real beef with the essential minerals needed for a happy and healthy life.**

**Veterinarians agree that this is the dog food to buy.**

• **Essential Minerals — Grade A Dog Chow** provides your dog with 12 essential minerals for good health. This means that **Grade A Dog Chow** has three more minerals than is recommended by the National Canine Council. For example, **Grade A Dog Chow** contains zinc for healthy skin, calcium for stronger bones, and sodium for proper kidney function.

• **Disease Protection — Grade A Dog Chow** is the first and only dog food that provides your dog with protection from heartworm. Heartworm medication is in the dog food. If your dog eats the recommended amount of food each day, he or she will receive the maximum protection needed to prevent this dreaded canine disease.

• **Real Beef — Grade A Dog Chow** contains real beef. Most dog foods are flavored with beef, but actually contain little or no real beef at all. Look at the list of ingredients on the container of your dog's food. If beef is not the first ingredient listed, then beef is not the main ingredient. We guarantee that **Grade A Dog Chow** is the only dog food on the market that lists beef first.

• **Convenient Packaging — Grade A Dog Chow** comes in convenient one-serving size cans or in 20-pound bags.

• **Great Price — Grade A Dog Chow** is the best dog food for your money. It is a reasonable $3.69 per pound.

We guarantee your dog will not only like our dog food, but eat it with gusto, or your money back!

GO ON

Name ________________________________ Date ________________

22. What is the author's mood in the first paragraph?
   (F) nervousness
   (G) boredom
   (H) irritation
   (J) enthusiasm

23. You can tell that the word *bilingual* means —
   (A) a number system based on 2.
   (B) having two languages.
   (C) wealthy.
   (D) a dry stream bed.

24. In the second journal entry, the phrase "made me feel claustrophobic" means the author was —
   (F) afraid of water.
   (G) willing to climb to great heights.
   (H) afraid of confined places.
   (J) used to traveling in boats.

25. Which is a *fact* expressed in the journal?
   (A) I love reading the street signs and food labels in French and English.
   (B) My favorite point of interest in the fort was the soldiers' barracks.
   (C) American Falls is higher than Horseshoe Falls.
   (D) The postcards sold at Niagara Falls are prettier than anywhere else on earth.

26. In the second journal entry, what word does the author use to mean "can't take my eyes off?"
   (F) mesmerizing
   (G) incredible
   (H) display
   (J) claustrophobic

27. In the third journal entry, the noise of Horseshoe Falls is compared to —
   (A) a boat.
   (B) noises in tunnels.
   (C) noise created by a whirlpool.
   (D) an approaching train.

28. Why was Fort Erie built?
   (F) as a supply depot and port
   (G) as a place for tourists to visit
   (H) as a lighthouse and store
   (J) as a place for the queen to live

29. The description of the soldiers' barracks at Fort Erie helps the reader know that —
   (A) the soldiers' families lived with them.
   (B) the soldiers were content at the fort.
   (C) the soldiers had many chores.
   (D) the soldiers were very uncomfortable.

30. What does the last journal entry describe?

________________________________________

________________________________________

________________________________________

________________________________________

31. What was the author's purpose in keeping this journal?

________________________________________

________________________________________

________________________________________

________________________________________

________________________________________

GO ON

Name ______________________ Date ______________

*NEW AND IMPROVED*

# Grade A Dog Chow

**A new and improved line of dog food that combines the flavor of real beef with the essential minerals needed for a happy and healthy life.**

**Veterinarians agree that this is the dog food to buy.**

• **Essential Minerals — Grade A Dog Chow** provides your dog with 12 essential minerals for good health. This means that **Grade A Dog Chow** has three more minerals than is recommended by the National Canine Council. For example, **Grade A Dog Chow** contains zinc for healthy skin, calcium for stronger bones, and sodium for proper kidney function.

• **Disease Protection — Grade A Dog Chow** is the first and only dog food that provides your dog with protection from heartworm. Heartworm medication is in the dog food. If your dog eats the recommended amount of food each day, he or she will receive the maximum protection needed to prevent this dreaded canine disease.

• **Real Beef — Grade A Dog Chow** contains real beef. Most dog foods are flavored with beef, but actually contain little or no real beef at all. Look at the list of ingredients on the container of your dog's food. If beef is not the first ingredient listed, then beef is not the main ingredient. We guarantee that **Grade A Dog Chow** is the only dog food on the market that lists beef first.

• **Convenient Packaging — Grade A Dog Chow** comes in convenient one-serving size cans or in 20-pound bags.

• **Great Price — Grade A Dog Chow** is the best dog food for your money. It is a reasonable $3.69 per pound.

We guarantee your dog will not only like our dog food, but eat it with gusto, or your money back!

GO ON

Name ______________________________ Date ______________

**32.** Which of these is a *fact* in the ad?

Ⓕ Grade A Dog Chow contains real beef.

Ⓖ Grade A Dog Chow is an improved line of dog food.

Ⓗ Dogs will like Grade A Dog Chow and eat it with gusto.

Ⓙ Grade A Dog Chow is the best dog food for your money.

**33.** There is enough information in the ad to show that —

Ⓐ phosphorus is harmful to your dog's health.

Ⓑ no other dog food is good for your dog.

Ⓒ Grade A Dog Chow contains several minerals.

Ⓓ Grade A Dog Chow is the only dog food recommended by pet-store owners.

**34.** The mineral in Grade A Dog Chow that helps with proper kidney function is —

Ⓕ selenium.

Ⓖ sodium.

Ⓗ zinc.

Ⓙ calcium.

**35.** The ad is meant to appeal to a desire to —

Ⓐ lower the fat in the diets of dogs.

Ⓑ increase the amount of fluids retained in dogs.

Ⓒ purchase dog food from veterinarians.

Ⓓ raise a happy dog that lives a long, healthy life.

**36.** According to the ad, beef is the main ingredient in dog food if —

Ⓕ it is flavored with beef.

Ⓖ beef is the first ingredient listed.

Ⓗ the food contains 12 essential minerals.

Ⓙ the containers are single-serving size.

**37.** What does the ad suggest about Grade A Dog Chow?

______________________________

______________________________

______________________________

______________________________

______________________________

______________________________

______________________________

______________________________

GO ON

Name ______________________________ Date ______________

## A Medical Pioneer

Today, if you need to have heart surgery, you can choose from many fine doctors. However, before 1893 this type of surgery was unknown. Doctors did not have modern medical tools and procedures essential for heart surgery, such as x-rays, antibiotics, and blood transfusions. In those days, heart patients were treated with sedatives, and they usually did not survive. Then in 1893, Daniel Hale Williams, a young African-American surgeon, attempted a new medical technique in order to save a patient's life.

One day a man named James Cornish was rushed to the emergency room in the hospital in Chicago where Dr. Williams worked. Cornish was suffering from a very serious knife wound. The knife had cut an artery less than an inch from Cornish's heart and punctured the pericardium, the sac around the heart. Dr. Williams called on six of his staff doctors to assist him with a complicated and daring operation. Dr. Williams became the first surgeon to save his patient by successfully repairing the human heart.

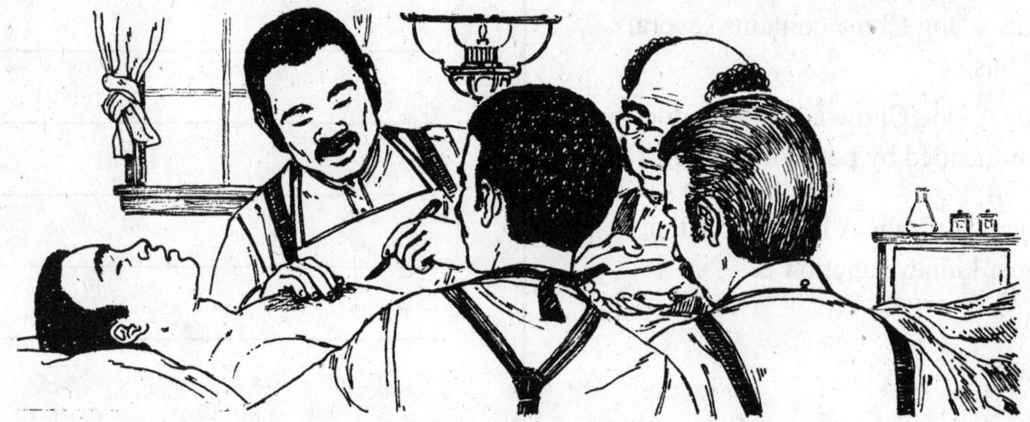

**38.** James Cornish is referred to as *patient* in the article because he —

Ⓐ does not lose his temper.

Ⓑ is under medical care.

Ⓒ is untiring.

Ⓓ does not complain about his problems.

**39.** Which of these would best help you understand this article?

Ⓕ finding Chicago, Illinois, on a map

Ⓖ looking up Daniel Hale Williams in an encyclopedia

Ⓗ looking up *antibiotics* in a dictionary

Ⓙ reading the history of modern medical tools

**40.** What happened to many heart patients before 1893?

Ⓐ They were x-rayed.

Ⓑ They died.

Ⓒ They had surgery.

Ⓓ They recovered.

**41.** What is another good title for this article?

______________________________

______________________________

______________________________

______________________________

STOP

Name ______________________________ Date ______________

# Test

**Sample A** **Polar Bears**

Polar bears are sometimes called ice bears or snow bears. These huge bears live in the icy lands near the North Pole. They sometimes weigh more than 1,000 pounds. Their thick, white fur and layers of fat help them stay warm in the freezing winters. Polar bears live by themselves except when a mother has cubs.

Why can polar bears live near the North Pole?

Ⓐ They build fires.

Ⓑ They huddle close together.

Ⓒ They stay in caves all winter.

Ⓓ They have thick fur and layers of fat.

**For questions 1–32, carefully read each selection and the questions that follow. Then darken the circle for the correct answer.**

## The World Food Crisis

In some parts of the world, food shortages cause many people to starve. Somehow, the world's food crop—the amount of food produced worldwide—must be increased. In order to help this happen, scientists have begun to study little-known, edible plants. There are about 20,000 kinds of edible plants, although only about 100 of them are grown as food crops.

Amaranth and leucaena are two plants that have the potential of becoming useful food crops in the near future. Amaranth is a grain that has been eaten in Mexico for hundreds of years. It can be grown in a variety of climates and soils, has many uses, and is rich in nutrients. Amaranth tastes good and can be ground and used as flour or popped like corn. Leucaena is a tree that may become a popular food source of the future. It can also be used for making fuel. This tall tree grows very fast.

As time goes on, more plants are being discovered and rediscovered. Scientists hope these plants will help solve the world's food crisis.

**1.** There is enough information in this article to show that —

Ⓐ meat will not be available in the future.

Ⓑ there are probably many useful edible plants that are not used as food crops.

Ⓒ leucaena is similar to broccoli.

Ⓓ amaranth probably will not be used very much as a food source in the future.

**2.** All are characteristics of the amaranth plant *except* —

Ⓕ it is used for making fuel.

Ⓖ it is rich in nutrients.

Ⓗ it tastes good.

Ⓙ it can be popped like corn.

**3.** What is this article mainly about?

______________________________

______________________________

Name ______________________________ Date ______________

# A Ride in an Airship

The first time I became interested in airships was when I read about the *Hindenburg* disaster. The *Hindenburg* was one of the largest airships ever built. It was about 804 feet long, 135 feet wide, and had a volume of 7,062,100 cubic feet. The *Hindenburg* was classified as a rigid airship. This kind of airship had a hull with a framework of wood or metal that supported the outer skin. Inside the hull were several gas cells that held hydrogen gas.

The *Hindenburg* was used for passenger service. There were 97 people aboard on May 6, 1937—the day it exploded while approaching its dock in Lakehurst, New Jersey. The disaster ended the development of rigid ships.

Today, there were three of us gathered who had won a contest at a local air show. Our prize was a ride in a blimp, or nonrigid airship. I was a bit *apprehensive* about accepting my prize, but I was very curious. When the blimp came to pick us up, it didn't land. Instead it remained a few feet above the ground, with its engines running. Even though the ground crew held the blimp steady with long ropes, it still moved around. I had to leap onto the stairway leading to the gondola.

Once inside the glass-enclosed gondola, I was comforted when I saw the two pilots, who appeared confident and relaxed. The dashboard was lit up with gauges and filled with switches. There were enough seats for six passengers. I chose a seat near the pilots and quickly latched my seat belt. Every passenger on board had a window seat. The windows on a blimp are much larger than the ones on jet airplanes. I could tell that this blimp was made for sightseeing.

As soon as everyone was seated, the pilots took the blimp to a height of about 2,500 feet. The best part of the ride was the view. Because blimps usually cruise at about 3,000 feet, or one tenth the height at which jets cruise, I could see things in detail. I could see traffic jams, people in swimming pools, and sculptures in open-air malls. The blimp flew over a football game for several minutes, and I could read the player's numbers! Since the cabin is not pressurized, I was able to open my window and wave to the people in the stands.

Once the pilots could see that their passengers were comfortable with their surroundings, they asked us if we were interested in learning more about the workings of a blimp. The pilots explained that the inside of the blimp's outer skin, or envelope, is filled with thousands of cubic feet of helium. Helium is lighter than air. When the helium in the envelope rises, it causes the blimp to ascend. Inside the envelope are two *ballonets,* one in front and one in back. These air-filled sacs help maintain the shape of the envelope. The pilots let air into or out of the ballonets during the flight to keep the pressure balanced in the envelope. The pilots demonstrated this to us. As the blimp gained altitude, helium pressure against the envelope increased. So the pilots let air out of the ballonets. Then, as the pilots moved the blimp downward to decrease altitude, the helium pressure against the envelope decreased. The pilots then let air into the ballonets.

After a short question-and-answer session with the pilots, we headed back to the airport. The pilots were in contact with the blimp's ground crew to make sure that they were ready for docking. As we approached the airfield, I thought about the *Hindenburg* as it prepared to dock on that fateful day in 1937. I reminded myself that helium, unlike hydrogen, is nonflammable. This helped calm me enough so that I could watch our docking. I counted 13 crew members on the field. They grabbed the two ropes that dangled from the nose of the blimp. I unbuckled my seat belt, thanked the pilots, and leaped out of the gondola and onto the ground.

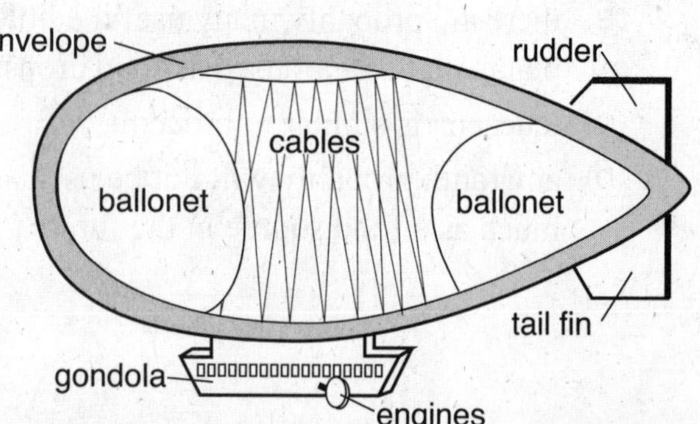


GO ON

Name ________________________________ Date ________________

4. What is the main idea of the first paragraph?

Ⓐ The *Hindenburg* was one of the largest airships ever built.

Ⓑ The *Hindenburg* was classified as a rigid airship.

Ⓒ The *Hindenburg* held hydrogen gas in its hull.

Ⓓ The *Hindenburg* disaster ended the development of rigid airships.

5. You can tell that the word *apprehensive* means —

Ⓕ nervous.

Ⓖ daring.

Ⓗ clever.

Ⓙ humorous.

6. You can tell from this article that the author views blimps with —

Ⓐ affection.

Ⓑ apprehension.

Ⓒ confidence.

Ⓓ indifference.

7. How did the author get into the gondola of the blimp?

_______________________________

_______________________________

_______________________________

_______________________________

_______________________________

_______________________________

_______________________________

8. Which expresses an *opinion* in the article?

Ⓕ The gondola on the blimp was glass-enclosed.

Ⓖ The best part of the blimp ride was the view.

Ⓗ Blimps cruise at about 3,000 feet.

Ⓙ A blimp's outer skin is called the envelope.

9. In this article, the author's fear of docking may have been caused by —

Ⓐ the question-and-answer session with the pilots.

Ⓑ the lack of ground crew members.

Ⓒ ropes dangling from the nose of the blimp.

Ⓓ knowledge of the *Hindenburg* disaster.

10. Which of these is a *fact* stated in the article?

Ⓕ Helium is nonflammable.

Ⓖ The pilots were confident.

Ⓗ People thought the *Hindenburg* was the greatest airship.

Ⓙ The author enjoyed waving to the people at the football game.

11. What is the purpose of ballonets on a blimp?

_______________________________

_______________________________

_______________________________

_______________________________

_______________________________

_______________________________

_______________________________

GO ON

Name ________________________________ Date ____________

# Gorillas—An Endangered Species

Gorillas are one of the many endangered species that live in Africa. These large fascinating apes are in danger of extinction for several reasons. As the human population of Africa grows, more land is needed for farmland. The rain forests where the gorillas live are being cut down to make new farms. In some regions, gorillas are hunted for meat.

**Western Lowland Gorilla**

There are three distinct groups of gorillas in Africa. The western lowland gorillas live in far west Africa near the equator. They make up the largest group, numbering between 35,000 and 45,000 individuals. These apes live in lowland forests and are mainly threatened by loss of habitat, as forests are cut down to make farms. Most gorillas in zoos are from western Africa.

**Eastern Lowland Gorilla**

The eastern lowland gorillas live in eastern Zaire. There are about 3,000 to 5,000 gorillas in this region. Like the western lowland gorillas, they are also threatened by the loss of their habitat. Poachers are another threat to the gorillas because the poachers roam the region, setting traps for deerlike animals called *duikers.* The poachers bend bamboo stalks and tie them to the ground. Then they attach a wire loop to the bamboo. When an animal steps into the loop, the bamboo springs up and jerks the animal off the ground. Often a gorilla can pull itself free from the trap, but the wire remains around its leg. The wound often becomes dirty and infected, causing the gorilla to sicken and die.

**Mountain Gorilla**

Mountain gorillas live in a small region on the border between Rwanda, Zaire, and Uganda. They live in an area 25 miles long and about 10 miles wide in the Virunga Mountains. Of the three kinds of gorillas, the mountain gorillas are the most endangered. There are fewer than 400 individuals left in the wild.

There is an encouraging side to the story of the mountain gorillas in Rwanda. Their home is protected because it is part of Rwanda's National Park of the Volcanoes. Because poachers were killing many gorillas, several large organizations banded together in 1978 to form the Mountain Gorilla Project. Its goals were to protect the park and to stop poaching. The project also aimed to increase tourism and to educate local people about gorillas.

Since 1978 the number of gorillas in the park has increased from 240 to nearly 300. Tourists from all over the world have come to see the gorillas. Trackers and tourist guides lead tourists deep into the mountains to observe the small bands of apes in their natural surroundings. Increased tourism has created jobs for many people in Rwanda. Tourism also provides money that can be used to catch poachers. The Mountain Gorilla Project teaches people about the value of the forest to the gorillas that live there.

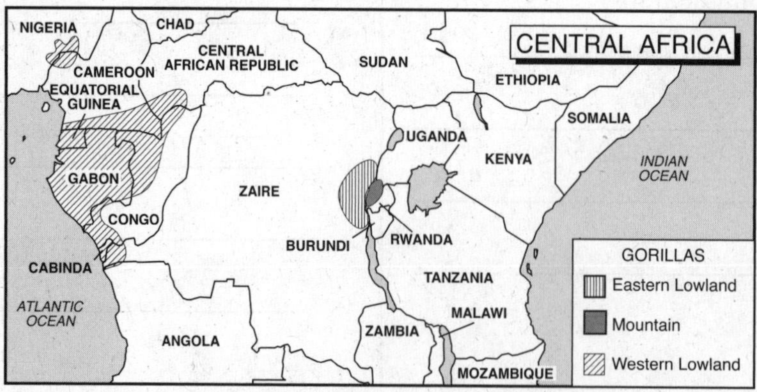


GO ON

Name ______________________________ Date ______________

12. This article would *most* likely be found in —

Ⓐ an English textbook.
Ⓑ a biography.
Ⓒ a nature magazine.
Ⓓ a science-fiction novel.

13. The web shows some important ideas in the article.

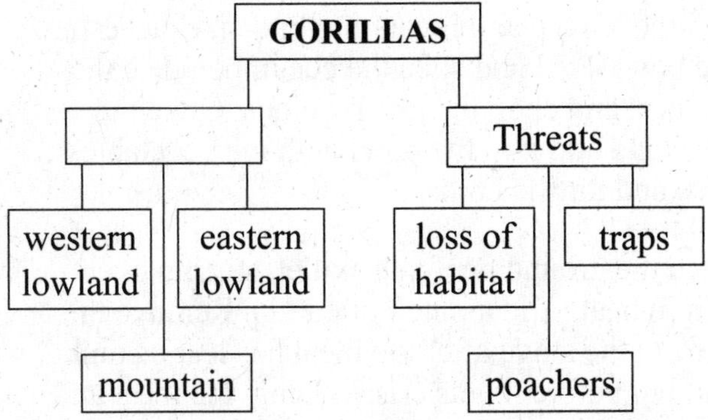


Which of these belongs in the empty space?

Ⓕ Reasons
Ⓖ Groups
Ⓗ Projects
Ⓙ Resources

14. Why are traps set for duikers dangerous to gorillas?

Ⓐ The wire from the trap wounds the gorilla, causing death.
Ⓑ Most gorillas cannot get out of the traps and they starve to death.
Ⓒ The gorillas are shot by poachers when they are found in the traps.
Ⓓ The traps poison the gorillas.

15. According to the map, where do the eastern lowland gorillas live?

Ⓕ in Rwanda
Ⓖ in Uganda
Ⓗ in Burundi
Ⓙ in Zaire

16. Several large organizations banded together to form the Mountain Gorilla Project because —

Ⓐ there were only five mountain gorillas left in the wild.
Ⓑ many gorillas were being killed by poachers.
Ⓒ gorillas were needed for zoos.
Ⓓ scientists wanted to visit the mountains and study the gorillas.

17. The last paragraph informs the reader —

Ⓕ about the habitat of the mountain gorilla.
Ⓖ about Rwanda's National Park of the Volcanoes.
Ⓗ about interactions between the eastern and western lowland gorillas.
Ⓙ about the success of the Mountain Gorilla Project.

18. Why is the rapidly growing human population in Africa a threat to the gorillas?

______________________________

______________________________

______________________________

______________________________

GO ON

Name ______________________________ Date ______________

# Jack's Night to Cook

On a hot summer day, nothing beats the flavor of spicy ground beef mixed with cheese, salsa, and cool vegetables. Jack located his favorite cookbook, *Simple Gourmet Cookbook,* and found the recipes he wanted to make. By following the instructions carefully, he made a delicious, well-balanced meal for himself and his family.

**Super Taco Salad** (serves 4)

**Ingredients:**

1 head lettuce

1 cucumber

1 pound ground beef

1 pinch cumin

1 15-ounce can of beans (kidney, black, green, or pinto)

2 medium tomatoes, diced

2 or 3 green onions, chopped

$1\frac{1}{2}$ cups tortilla chips

$1\frac{2}{3}$ cups cheese, grated (either Monterey Jack or mild Cheddar)

$\frac{1}{4}$ cup sour cream (optional)

$\frac{1}{4}$ cup salad dressing (see page 97)

$\frac{1}{4}$ cup salsa (see page 105)

Wash the lettuce and break into bite-size pieces in a large bowl. Peel and slice the cucumber, dice the tomatoes, and chop the green onions. Grate the cheese and add it to the bowl with the vegetables, beans, and tortilla chips.

Brown the ground beef in a skillet, stirring over medium heat. Add a pinch of cumin. Remove the pan from the stove after the meat has lost its pink color, but before it gets crispy. Drain the meat and add it to the salad.

Add the salad dressing, and toss the salad well. For a spicier flavor, blend in the salsa. Finally, add the sour cream and garnish the top of the salad with more tortilla chips.

**Salsa**

**Ingredients:**

2 ripe tomatoes, diced

1 small onion, chopped fine

$\frac{1}{2}$ teaspoon finely chopped chiles (fresh or canned)

Salt and pepper to taste

Dice the tomatoes, and chop the onions and chiles. Combine all ingredients in a small bowl.

**Salad Dressing**

**Ingredients:**

In a small bowl or jar, combine the following —

1 teaspoon lemon juice or vinegar

3 tablespoons olive oil or vegetable oil

$\frac{1}{4}$ teaspoon dry mustard (optional)

Salt and pepper to taste

Mix or shake ingredients to blend. Refrigerate. Shake well before using.

GO ON

Name ______________________________ Date ______________

19. Jack needs all the following things to make the Super Taco Salad *except* —

Ⓐ a fork.

Ⓑ a skillet.

Ⓒ a can opener.

Ⓓ a grater.

20. Which ingredient does Jack need in order to make both the taco salad and the salsa?

Ⓕ cheese

Ⓖ green onions

Ⓗ tomatoes

Ⓙ chiles

21. How much cheese should Jack add to the taco salad?

Ⓐ $1\frac{1}{2}$ cups

Ⓑ $1\frac{1}{4}$ teaspoons

Ⓒ $1\frac{2}{3}$ cups

Ⓓ $\frac{1}{3}$ teaspoon

22. What is the first thing Jack does when making the taco salad?

Ⓕ grates the cheese

Ⓖ opens the can of beans

Ⓗ washes the lettuce

Ⓙ slices the cucumber

23. According to the recipe, when should Jack add the salad dressing to the taco salad?

Ⓐ before he browns the ground beef

Ⓑ after he garnishes the salad with tortilla chips

Ⓒ after he adds the meat to the salad

Ⓓ before he adds the beans to the salad

24. How does Jack prepare the green onions for the taco salad?

Ⓕ He slices them.

Ⓖ He chops them.

Ⓗ He browns them.

Ⓙ He grates them.

25. If Jack discovers he is out of olive oil, what can he use instead?

Ⓐ vinegar

Ⓑ vegetable oil

Ⓒ lemon juice

Ⓓ dry mustard

26. What should Jack do just after he adds the salad dressing to the salad?

Ⓕ Shake the jar.

Ⓖ Add more lemon juice.

Ⓗ Stir it over medium heat.

Ⓙ Toss the salad well.

27. Where can Jack find the recipe for salad dressing in *Simple Gourmet Cooking?*

Ⓐ page 24

Ⓑ page 97

Ⓒ page 105

Ⓓ page 211

28. Why are these recipes good for a hot summer day?

______________________________

______________________________

______________________________

______________________________

GO ON

Name ______________________________ Date ______________

## Attic Finds

My brother Paul and I helped our mom clean out the attic the other day. We hoped to find a shoe box full of baseball cards from the 1960s that our dad collected when he was about our age. We figured that if the cards were in perfect condition, they might be worth hundreds of dollars.

The first box that we came upon contained holiday decorations that my great-grandmother had given my mother years ago. Every one of the decorations was handmade, and we marveled at the amount of time it must have taken to make each one. Mom had stories about some of the pieces—tales passed down to her by her grandmother.

Finally we found a shoe box that fit the description that Dad had given us. I undid the rubber band so fast that it shot into the other side of the attic. What I found inside wasn't what I had hoped for and expected, but something more valuable to our family than cards of baseball celebrities. I discovered a shoe box full of yellowing letters. The bottom of each page had an odd typed message, "Help our country by saving. Write on BOTH sides of this paper." The top of each paper had a United States flag in the upper left-hand corner, a triangle with the letters *YMCA* in the upper right-hand corner, and the typed words *With the Colors* in the middle of the page. Upon further inspection, Paul and I realized that we had a collection of letters written by our great-uncle Frank while he served as a bugler in the United States Army during World War I. His letters started in boot camp in 1917 and ended in France in 1918. Paul and I spent the rest of the day mulling over the letters.

**29.** The author assumes the reader already knows —

- Ⓕ why he and his brother are cleaning the attic.
- Ⓖ who gave his mother the holiday decorations.
- Ⓗ what a boot camp is.
- Ⓙ when the letters were written.

**30.** Why was the message put on the bottom of each page of the letters?

______________________________

______________________________

______________________________

______________________________

**31.** Based on the article, you can tell that the author probably —

- Ⓐ threw away the letters.
- Ⓑ read each letter.
- Ⓒ left the letters in the attic.
- Ⓓ sold the letters to a collector.

**32.** The third paragraph tells mainly —

- Ⓕ what baseball cards were found in the box.
- Ⓖ about finding something unexpected in an attic.
- Ⓗ why World War I started.
- Ⓙ how the United States Army won World War I.

STOP

Name ______________________________ Date ______________

# Unit 4: Reading Vocabulary

## DETERMINING WORD MEANINGS

**Directions: Darken the circle for the word or group of words that has the same or almost the same meaning as the underlined word.**

| **Try This** | Choose your answer carefully. The other choices may seem correct. Be sure to think about the meaning of the underlined word. |
|---|---|

**Sample A**

To <u>transmit</u> is to —

Ⓐ imprint.
Ⓑ design.
Ⓒ interpret.
Ⓓ send.

| **Think It Through** | The correct answer is <u>D</u>, "send." <u>Transmit</u> means "send." It doesn't mean imprint, design, or interpret. |
|---|---|

1. Something that is <u>adjacent</u> is —
   Ⓐ crumbling.
   Ⓑ locked.
   Ⓒ neighboring.
   Ⓓ illegal.

2. <u>Conspicuous</u> means —
   Ⓕ invisible.
   Ⓖ considerate.
   Ⓗ adequate.
   Ⓙ obvious.

3. A <u>caress</u> is a kind of —
   Ⓐ soap.
   Ⓑ cloth.
   Ⓒ touch.
   Ⓓ word.

4. Something that is <u>hazardous</u> is —
   Ⓕ guarded.
   Ⓖ chemical.
   Ⓗ scenic.
   Ⓙ perilous.

5. A <u>rebellion</u> is —
   Ⓐ a border.
   Ⓑ a conference.
   Ⓒ an uprising.
   Ⓓ an organization.

6. To <u>merge</u> is to —
   Ⓕ unite.
   Ⓖ veer.
   Ⓗ obstruct.
   Ⓙ anticipate.

7. Someone who is in <u>agony</u> is in —
   Ⓐ traction.
   Ⓑ sadness.
   Ⓒ great pain.
   Ⓓ a forest.

8. To <u>categorize</u> is to —
   Ⓕ classify.
   Ⓖ describe.
   Ⓗ analyze.
   Ⓙ respond.

9. <u>Vast</u> is the same as —
   Ⓐ green.
   Ⓑ wild.
   Ⓒ enormous.
   Ⓓ settled.

10. To <u>veto</u> is to —
    Ⓕ forbid.
    Ⓖ like.
    Ⓗ suggest.
    Ⓙ order.

STOP

Name ______________________________ Date ______________

# MATCHING WORDS WITH MORE THAN ONE MEANING

**Directions: Darken the circle for the sentence that uses the underlined word in the same way as the sentence in the box.**

| **Try This** | Read the sentence in the box. Decide what the underlined word means. Then find the sentence in which the underlined word has the same meaning. |
|---|---|

**Sample A**

> What is the current temperature?

In which sentence does current have the same meaning as it does in the sentence above?

Ⓐ The river's strong current washed the pier away.
Ⓑ Our class discusses current events.
Ⓒ The current of the oceans creates a pattern across the face of the earth.
Ⓓ How is an electric current produced?

| **Think It Through** | The correct answer is B. In choice B and in the sentence in the box, current means "present." |
|---|---|

STOP

**1.**

> The date of the next track meet is March 5, 2002.

In which sentence does date have the same meaning as it does in the sentence above?

Ⓐ Scientists use carbon dating to date fossils.
Ⓑ Will Mary be Jesse's date for the dance?
Ⓒ The date palm produces a sweet fruit.
Ⓓ What is today's date?

**2.**

> Megan was elected class delegate.

In which sentence does delegate have the same meaning as it does in the sentence above?

Ⓕ Our state delegate just resigned.
Ⓖ The teacher will delegate two students to make copies of the program.
Ⓗ The Constitution provides for citizens to delegate power to their elected representatives.
Ⓙ You need to delegate some of your responsibilities to others.

**3.**

> During a depression many people lose their jobs.

In which sentence does depression have the same meaning as it does in the sentence above?

Ⓐ The boulder that fell from the cliff made a depression in the ground.
Ⓑ He often suffers from depression.
Ⓒ The depression you see is the result of a meteor that crashed to the earth.
Ⓓ When the depression ended, the economy started improving.

**4.**

> Where is the river's outlet?

In which sentence does outlet have the same meaning as it does in the sentence above?

Ⓕ Please find the electrical outlet.
Ⓖ You need an outlet for your energy.
Ⓗ The mud slide blocked the outlet from the campground.
Ⓙ Let's shop at the new shoe outlet.

Name ______________________ Date ______________

# USING CONTEXT CLUES

**Directions: Darken the circle for the word or words that give the meaning of the underlined word.**

| **Try This** | Read the first sentence carefully. Look for clue words in the sentence. Then use each answer choice in place of the underlined word. Be sure that your answer and the underlined word have the same meaning. |
|---|---|

**Sample A**

During the strike the factory was empty, and the machines were idle. Idle means —

Ⓐ busy. Ⓑ operating. Ⓒ occupied. Ⓓ inactive.

| **Think It Through** | The correct answer is D. Idle means "inactive." The clue words are "empty" and "strike." The three other choices mean the opposite of idle. |
|---|---|

1. Nurse Gibbons praised Kyle for being a very efficient hospital volunteer. Efficient means —
   Ⓐ talkative. Ⓑ capable. Ⓒ irritating. Ⓓ slow.

2. To prevent infection, it is extremely important that hospitals be hygienic. Hygienic means —
   Ⓕ organized. Ⓖ charitable. Ⓗ sanitary. Ⓙ thrifty.

3. Alexandra felt annoyed because she was tired of waiting in the slow cafeteria line. Annoyed means —
   Ⓐ afraid. Ⓑ silly. Ⓒ fearless. Ⓓ bothered.

4. The students voted to abolish the unpopular dress code. Abolish means —
   Ⓕ preserve. Ⓖ eliminate. Ⓗ promote. Ⓙ hide.

5. The man was convicted for his reprehensible acts. Reprehensible means —
   Ⓐ courageous. Ⓑ disgraceful. Ⓒ thoughtful. Ⓓ courteous.

6. The rustler was a hated figure in the Wild West. Rustler means —
   Ⓕ cattle thief. Ⓖ sheriff. Ⓗ ranch hand. Ⓙ cowboy.

7. At the climax of the movie, the hero faced his deadly adversary. Adversary means —
   Ⓐ friend. Ⓑ companion. Ⓒ enemy. Ⓓ leader.

8. Alyssa loves the incredible stories about mythical figures. Mythical means —
   Ⓕ imaginary. Ⓖ heroic. Ⓗ strange. Ⓙ military.

STOP

Name ______________________ Date ______________

# Test

**Sample A**

To convey is to —

Ⓐ build.

Ⓑ transport.

Ⓒ examine.

Ⓓ memorize.

STOP

**For questions 1–8, darken the circle for the word or group of words that has the same or almost the same meaning as the underlined word.**

1. To defy is to —

Ⓐ expose.

Ⓑ support.

Ⓒ challenge.

Ⓓ excuse.

2. Absurd means —

Ⓕ admirable.

Ⓖ confused.

Ⓗ forgotten.

Ⓙ ridiculous.

3. A replica is —

Ⓐ an experiment.

Ⓑ a secret code.

Ⓒ an exact copy.

Ⓓ a priceless antique.

4. Something that is amiss is —

Ⓕ filthy.

Ⓖ satisfactory.

Ⓗ lost.

Ⓙ wrong.

5. Dense means —

Ⓐ thick.

Ⓑ smoky.

Ⓒ dirty.

Ⓓ dangerous.

6. An inquiry is —

Ⓕ a delivery.

Ⓖ an identity.

Ⓗ an investigation.

Ⓙ a route.

7. A pamphlet is a kind of —

Ⓐ teacher.

Ⓑ academy.

Ⓒ newspaper.

Ⓓ booklet.

8. To allay is to —

Ⓕ put at rest.

Ⓖ discuss in public.

Ⓗ make fun of.

Ⓙ imagine.

**Write your answer for the following:**

9. What is the meaning of the word aroma?

______________________________

______________________________

______________________________

______________________________

GO ON

Name ____________________ Date ____________

**Sample B**

| The hiker tried to scale the mountain. |
|---|

In which sentence does scale have the same meaning as it does in the sentence above?

Ⓐ Find the distance scale on the map.

Ⓑ He can easily scale that wall.

Ⓒ The doctor carefully placed the newborn baby on the scale.

Ⓓ What is the pay scale for this job?

**For questions 10–14, darken the circle for the sentence in which the underlined word means the same as it does in the sentence in the box.**

**10.** Kaitlin is helping Rodney build a new pen for the cattle.

In which sentence does pen have the same meaning as it does in the sentence above?

Ⓐ How did the pigs get out of their pen?

Ⓑ May I please borrow your pen?

Ⓒ Where is Dad going to pen the sheep?

Ⓓ Why did that author pen such an awful book?

**11.** There was a remote possibility that she was telling the truth.

In which sentence does remote have the same meaning as it does in the sentence above?

Ⓕ Where did you put the remote control?

Ⓖ He is a remote ancestor of mine.

Ⓗ The house was located in a remote part of town.

Ⓙ They had a remote chance of winning the contest.

**12.** The teacher will marshal the children out of the building.

In which sentence does marshal have the same meaning as it does in the sentence above?

Ⓐ He was once a federal marshal.

Ⓑ It would be best to marshal your arguments in order of importance.

Ⓒ She is the new city fire marshal.

Ⓓ marshal them into a single file.

**13.** Dad helped me review for the Spanish test.

In which sentence does review have the same meaning as it does in the sentence above?

Ⓕ The general requested a review of the troops before the ceremony.

Ⓖ He wrote a very glowing review of her latest novel.

Ⓗ The musical review was a great success.

Ⓙ The detectives met to review the events that led to the crime.

**14.** Mom can maneuver the car through heavy traffic easily.

In which sentence does maneuver have the same meaning as it does in the sentence above?

Ⓐ Pilots learn to maneuver their planes in emergency situations.

Ⓑ The movement of thousands of troops in an hour was a huge maneuver.

Ⓒ The soldiers practiced the maneuver all weekend.

Ⓓ She can maneuver her way out of any uncomfortable situation.

GO ON

Name ____________________ Date ____________

**Sample C**

The cost for the car repair was trivial. Trivial means —

Ⓐ insignificant.
Ⓑ necessary.
Ⓒ important.
Ⓓ expensive.

**For questions 15–22, darken the circle for the word or words that give the meaning of the underlined word.**

**15.** The detectives were totally baffled by the lack of clues in the case. Baffled means —

Ⓕ puzzled.
Ⓖ rewarded.
Ⓗ amused.
Ⓙ relaxed.

**16.** Carol tried to remain neutral while her two friends argued. Neutral means —

Ⓐ giving advice.
Ⓑ not taking sides.
Ⓒ perfectly still.
Ⓓ whistling.

**17.** Tree limbs and branches scattered by the storm obstructed the entrance to the park. Obstructed means —

Ⓕ blocked.
Ⓖ signaled.
Ⓗ opened.
Ⓙ decorated.

**18.** Dale was coughing and sneezing, and he felt altogether miserable. Miserable means —

Ⓐ energetic.
Ⓑ starved.
Ⓒ unhappy.
Ⓓ generous.

**19.** My dog Skipper is notorious for chewing anything, but he is especially fond of shoes. Notorious means —

Ⓕ pampered.
Ⓖ remorseful.
Ⓗ abnormal.
Ⓙ well-known.

**20.** Many people leave their countries to escape political oppression. Oppression means —

Ⓐ freedom.
Ⓑ benefits.
Ⓒ persecution.
Ⓓ reliability.

**21.** That scoundrel stole the widower's life savings. What is the meaning of the word scoundrel?

______________________________

______________________________

______________________________

**22.** It is important that the researchers keep a sanitary laboratory. What is the meaning of the word sanitary?

______________________________

______________________________

______________________________

STOP

Name ______________________________ Date ______________

# Unit 5: Math Problem-Solving Strategies

## OVERVIEW

### The Problem-Solving Plan

*When solving math problems follow these steps:*

**STEP 1: WHAT IS THE QUESTION/GOAL?**

Read the problem. Decide what must be found. This is sometimes in the form of a question.

**STEP 2: FIND THE FACTS**

Locate the factual information in three different ways:

**A.** **KEY FACTS**...the facts you need to solve the problem.

**B.** **FACTS YOU DON'T NEED**...those facts that are not necessary for solving the problem.

**C.** **ARE MORE FACTS NEEDED?**...decide if you have enough information to solve the problem. If not, what information would you need or what assumptions could you make to arrive at a conclusion?

**STEP 3: SELECT A STRATEGY**

Decide what strategies you might use, how you will use them, and in what form you will offer your solution. For example, will you present your solution numerically, in words, in a chart or diagram, or in some other way? If one strategy doesn't help you to solve the problem, try another.

**STEP 4: SOLVE**

Apply the strategy according to your plan. Communicate your solution in a clear and accurate fashion.

**STEP 5: DOES YOUR RESPONSE MAKE SENSE?**

Think about your solution. Read the problem again. Check to see that your answer makes sense. Use estimation to check calculations.

Name ______________________________ Date ______________

## PROBLEM 1

**PROBLEM/QUESTION:**

Migdalia is a consultant. She works 3 days a week in the company's headquarters and 2 days a week at a production site. When she works at the company headquarters, she takes a bus to and from work. When she goes to production sites, she uses her car and travels 52 miles per day. The cost for using the bus is $48.00 for 10 one-way trips. The cost of using her car she estimates at 30¢ per mile. Migdalia budgets $50 per week for travel expenses to and from work. Show whether or not she has set aside enough money.

**STEP 1: WHAT IS THE QUESTION/GOAL?**

**STEP 2: FIND THE FACTS**

**STEP 3: SELECT A STRATEGY**

**STEP 4: SOLVE**

**STEP 5: DOES YOUR RESPONSE MAKE SENSE?**

Name ____________________ Date ____________________

## PROBLEM 2

### PROBLEM/QUESTION:

Alberto has an L-shaped room shown in the diagram at the right. He has purchased a square piece of carpeting which has an area of 30 sq. yds. Approximately what percent of the carpet he purchased will be left over?

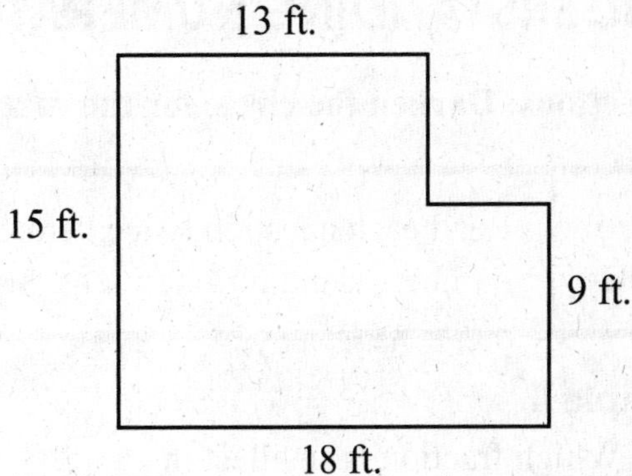


### STEP 1: WHAT IS THE QUESTION/GOAL?

### STEP 2: FIND THE FACTS

### STEP 3: SELECT A STRATEGY

### STEP 4: SOLVE

### STEP 5: DOES YOUR RESPONSE MAKE SENSE?

Name ________________________________ Date ______________

# Unit 6: Math Problem Solving

## UNDERSTANDING NUMERATION

**Directions: Darken the circle for the correct answer, or write in the answer.**

| **Try This** | Read each question twice before choosing your answer. Be sure to think about which numbers stand for ones, tens, hundreds, and so on. |
|---|---|

**Sample A**

Which fraction is smallest in value?

Ⓐ $\frac{1}{8}$　　Ⓒ $\frac{3}{5}$

Ⓑ $\frac{1}{5}$　　Ⓓ $\frac{3}{8}$

| **Think It Through** | The correct answer is A. The fraction $\frac{1}{8}$ is smaller than the other fractions listed. If you use the common denominator 40, $\frac{1}{8}$ becomes $\frac{5}{40}$, but the other fractions become $\frac{8}{40}$, $\frac{24}{40}$, and $\frac{15}{40}$. |
|---|---|

**1.** Oceanographers estimate that the Atlantic Ocean covers $4.1 \times 10^7$ square miles, expressed in scientific notation. What is another way that number can be written?

Ⓐ 410 square miles

Ⓑ 41,000 square miles

Ⓒ 410,000 square miles

Ⓓ 41,000,000 square miles

**2.** What is the value of point B on the number line?

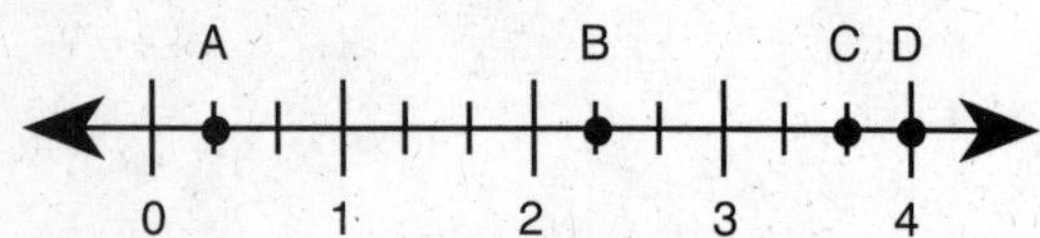


Ⓕ 4　　Ⓗ $2\frac{1}{3}$

Ⓖ $3\frac{2}{3}$　　Ⓙ $\frac{1}{3}$

**3.** Which decimal equals $\frac{7}{20}$?

Ⓐ 0.35　　Ⓒ 0.7

Ⓑ 7.20　　Ⓓ 0.14

**4.** Which fraction is not equivalent to the others in the group?

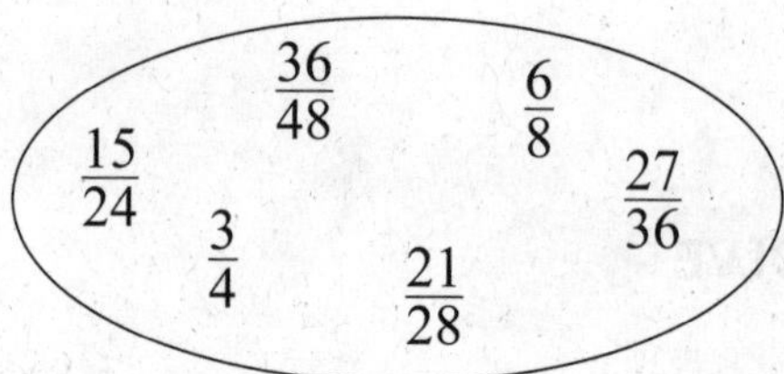


Ⓕ $\frac{6}{8}$　　Ⓗ $\frac{3}{4}$

Ⓖ $\frac{15}{24}$　　Ⓙ $\frac{27}{36}$

**5.** Which of these is a composite number?

Ⓐ 3　　Ⓒ 12

Ⓑ 11　　Ⓓ 19

**6.** Yesterday in Yukon City the temperature was –4°F. Today, the temperature rose 6 degrees. What is the temperature today?

______________________________

______________________________

GO ON

7. Maddy saw this sign when she was shopping. What is the value of the 5 in the sale price of men's ties?

Felt Hats
$21.50 each
Reg. $30.00
Long Sleeve T-Shirts
$7.00 each
Reg. $15.00
Many colors
Gloves and Mittens
Knit mittens...$6.00
Leather gloves...$15.00
Ski gloves...$14.00
Special Group of Dresses
originally $53.00
Now 1/2 off
Sweaters
All colors and patterns
Were $25.00
Now $18.50
Dress Shirts
Were $35.00
Now $21.00
Men's Ties
$9.75 each
Limited supply


Ⓕ 5 thousandths
Ⓖ 5 hundredths
Ⓗ 5 tenths
Ⓙ 5 ones

8. Which bag of dog food pictured here weighs the least?

Bag A

Doggie Grub

$4\frac{2}{3}$ lb.

Bag C

Bag B

Gourmet Dog Food

$4\frac{3}{4}$ lb.

Bag D

Ⓐ Bag A
Ⓑ Bag B
Ⓒ Bag C
Ⓓ Bag D

9. Which number is <u>not</u> a prime number?

Ⓕ 11
Ⓖ 17
Ⓗ 27
Ⓙ 31

10. Each □ represents 0.001. Which number is represented in the picture shown here?

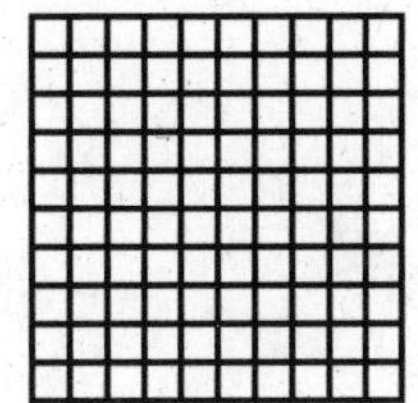

Ⓐ 12.5
Ⓑ 1.25
Ⓒ 0.125
Ⓓ 0.0125

11. Which scale is correctly balanced?

Ⓕ
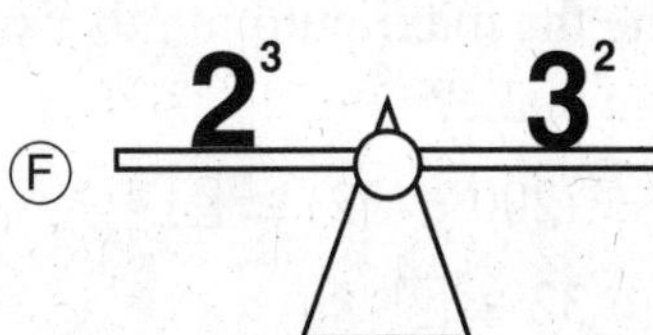


Ⓖ
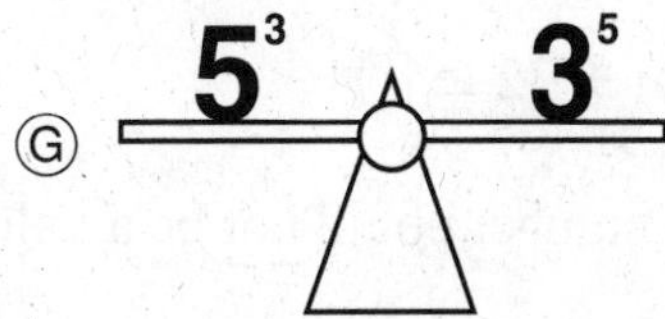


Ⓗ
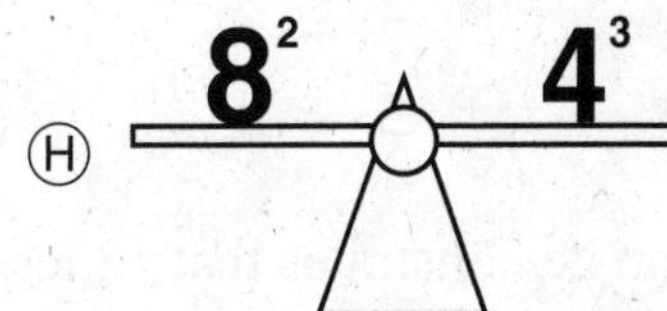


Ⓙ
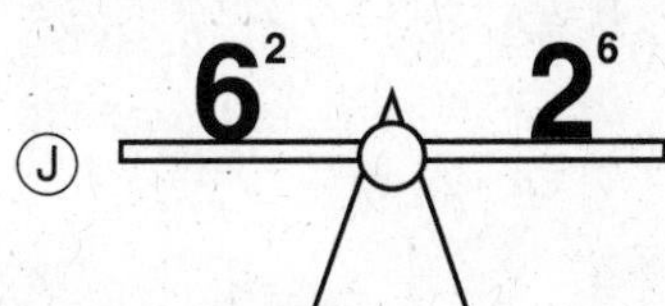


STOP

Name ______________________ Date ______________

# UNDERSTANDING ALGEBRA

**Directions: Darken the circle for the correct answer, or write in your answer.**

| **Try This** | Check your work by making sure both sides of an equation are equal values. Try using all the answer choices in the problem. |
|---|---|

**Sample A**

If $x > y$ and $y > z$, then

Ⓐ $x < z$  Ⓒ $x = z$

Ⓑ $x \geq z$  Ⓓ $x > z$

| **Think It Through** | The correct answer is D. If ***x*** is greater than ***y***, and ***y*** is greater than *z*, it is logical that ***x*** is also greater than *z*. |
|---|---|

STOP

1. Holly is making 2 kinds of necklaces. For one, she uses blue beads. For the other, she uses green beads. She needs 32 beads for each necklace. If she has 300 blue beads and 200 green beads, which number sentence could be used to determine the maximum number of necklaces she can make?

   Ⓐ $(300 \div 32) + (200 \div 32) \geq \square$

   Ⓑ $300 + 200 + 32 \geq \square$

   Ⓒ $300 \geq \square \div 32$

   Ⓓ $(300 - 200) \div 32 \geq \square$

2. If $5 > y$, which number could not be a value for $y$?

   Ⓕ $-4$  Ⓗ 4

   Ⓖ 2  Ⓙ 5

3. Which expression demonstrates that 12 less than $x$ equals 40?

   Ⓐ $12 \div x = 40$

   Ⓑ $12 - x = 40$

   Ⓒ $40 - 12 \leq x$

   Ⓓ $x - 12 = 40$

4. Mei baked a German chocolate cake. She knows that the cake contains 2,700 calories. She has cut the cake into 12 equal-size slices. Write an equation to determine the number of calories in each slice.

   ______________________________

   ______________________________

5. Mr. Lopez bought 3 boxes of cereal for \$2.65 each. He bought 6 cartons of orange juice for \$0.89 each. Which number sentence could be used to determine how much money Mr. Lopez spent altogether?

   Ⓕ $(3 \times \$2.65) + (6 \times \$0.89) = \square$

   Ⓖ $(\$2.65 + \$0.89) \times (3 + 6) = \square$

   Ⓗ $(3 \times 6) + (\$2.65 \times \$0.89) = \square$

   Ⓙ $(3 + \$2.65) \times (6 + \$0.89) = \square$

STOP

Name ____________________ Date ____________

## WORKING WITH PATTERNS AND FUNCTIONS

**Directions: Darken the circle for the correct answer, or write in your answer.**

| **Try This** | Read each problem carefully. Determine the nature of the pattern or relationship in the problem. Try using all the answer choices in the problem to find the correct solution. |
|---|---|

**Sample A**

Rodney is saving money to buy his first car. His parents agreed to contribute 50 cents for every dollar he saved. If he has saved $1,100, how much can he afford to spend on the car?

Ⓐ $1450
Ⓑ $1650
Ⓒ $2300
Ⓓ $3450

| **Think It Through** | The correct answer is B. If Rodney has saved $1100, then his parents are contributing half of the $1100, or $550. Therefore, Rodney can afford to spend $1100 + $550, or $1650, on the car. |
|---|---|

1. A special machine multiplies any number entered into it by 8. The table shows how numbers are changed. Which numbers are missing from the table? Write them in the empty boxes.

| Original number | 5 | 7 | 10 |
|---|---|---|---|
| New number | 40 | | |

2. If 3 teaspoons of baking powder are required for a batch of 8 pancakes, how much baking powder will be needed for a batch of 32 pancakes?

Ⓐ 6 teaspoons
Ⓑ 8 teaspoons
Ⓒ 9 teaspoons
Ⓓ 12 teaspoons

3. Look at the part of Pascal's Triangle shown here. What would the next line be if the pattern continues?

**1**
**1 1**
**1 2 1**
**1 3 3 1**
**1 4 6 4 1**
**1 5 10 10 5 1**

Ⓕ 1 5 15 1 5 1
Ⓖ 1 6 15 20 15 6 1
Ⓗ 1 7 16 16 7 1
Ⓙ 1 6 12 24 12 6 1

STOP

Name ______________________________ Date ______________

# UNDERSTANDING PROBABILITY AND STATISTICS

**Directions: Darken the circle for the correct answer, or write in your answer.**

| **Try This** | Read each question twice before choosing your answer. Study any given tables or graphs to help you choose the correct answer. |
|---|---|

**Sample A**

Two coins are tossed into the air. What is the probability that they will match either heads-heads or tails-tails when they land?

Ⓐ $\frac{1}{1}$

Ⓑ $\frac{1}{2}$

Ⓒ $\frac{1}{4}$

Ⓓ $\frac{1}{8}$

| **Think It Through** | The correct answer is B. There are four possibilities: heads-heads, tails-tails, heads-tails, and tails-heads. Two of these four possibilities will match. That makes the correct answer a probability of $\frac{2}{4}$, or $\frac{1}{2}$ |
|---|---|

1. The graph depicts the rainfall in a city over a 12-month period.

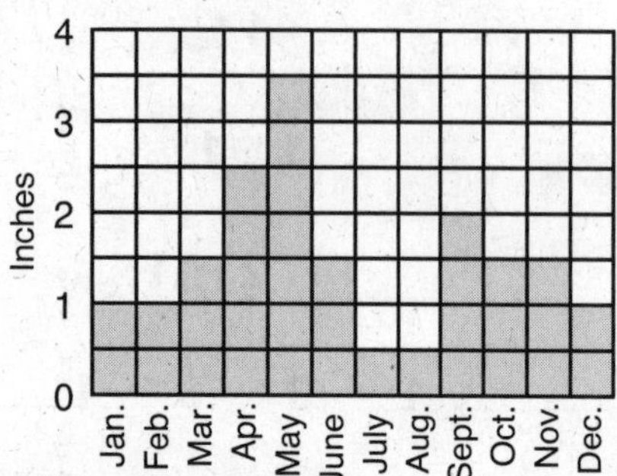


Which of these statements is true, based on the information in the graph?

Ⓐ There were 18 inches of rainfall during the 12-month period shown on the graph.

Ⓑ It rained 2 inches in December.

Ⓒ There was more rainfall in April and in May than in the rest of the months combined.

Ⓓ There was less rainfall in November than in any other month of the year.

2. The graph shows the results of a student vote taken to select the music for a school dance. If 600 students voted, how many voted for rock music?

Ⓕ 560

Ⓖ 340

Ⓗ 240

Ⓙ 142

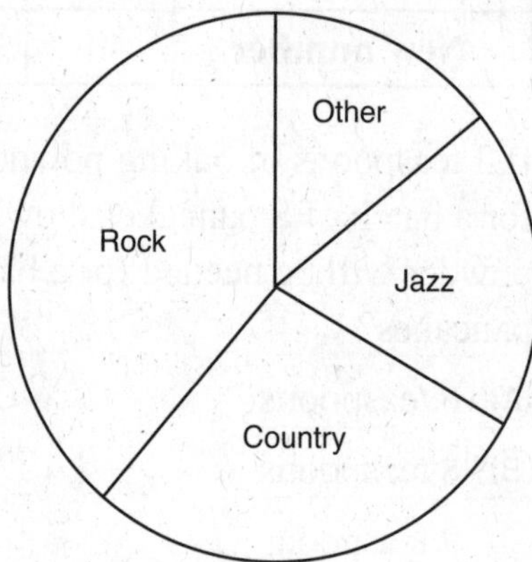


GO ON

Name ____________________ Date ____________

**A stem-and-leaf chart is an easy method of organizing data from a list.**

| Stem | Leaf |
|---|---|
| 15 | 2,4,6 |
| 16 | 2,3 |

means

| 152, 154, 156 |
|---|
| 162, 163 |

**The stem-and-leaf chart below shows the finishing times (in seconds) for the 100-meter dash at a recent middle school track meet. Use the chart to answer questions 3 through 5.**

| Finishing Times (in seconds) | |
|---|---|
| **Stem** | **Leaf** |
| 12 | 8, 9 |
| 13 | 6, 7, 9, 9 |
| 14 | 2, 8 |
| 15 | 2, 7 |

3. Which tally chart shows the correct finishing times shown in the chart above?

Ⓐ

| 120 - 130 | \|\| |
|---|---|
| 130 - 140 | \|\|\|\| |
| 140 - 150 | \|\| |
| 150 - 160 | \|\| |

Ⓒ

| 120 - 130 | \|\|\| |
|---|---|
| 130 - 140 | \|\|\|\| |
| 140 - 150 | \|\|\| |
| 150 - 160 | \|\|\| |

Ⓑ

| 120 - 130 | \|\|\| |
|---|---|
| 130 - 140 | \|\|\|\| |
| 140 - 150 | \| |
| 150 - 160 | \|\| |

Ⓓ

| 120 - 130 | \|\|\| |
|---|---|
| 130 - 140 | \|\|\|\| |
| 140 - 150 | \|\|\| |
| 150 - 160 | \|\| |

4. What is the probability that a student's time was less than 140 seconds?

Ⓕ $\frac{1}{10}$ Ⓗ $\frac{2}{5}$

Ⓖ $\frac{1}{4}$ Ⓙ $\frac{3}{5}$

5. How many students had a finishing time greater than 137 seconds?

Ⓐ 8 Ⓒ 6

Ⓑ 7 Ⓓ 5

6. Tanya made each point on the scatter plot represent test results. The coordinates for each point show the hours she studied for the test and the grade she received.

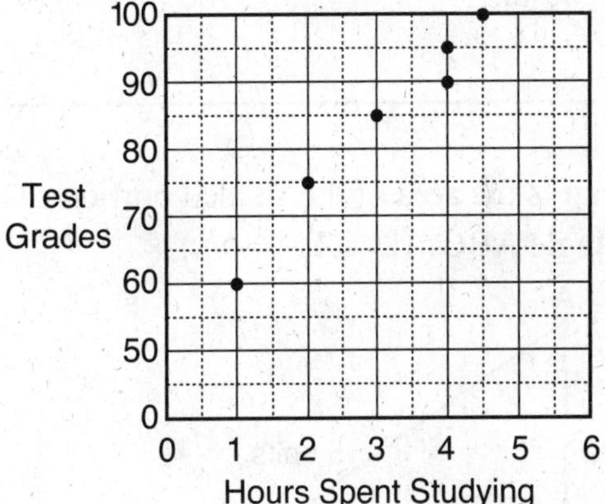


How many hours did Tanya study to receive a grade of 90?

____________________

____________________

7. If 45 out of 100 people said that they read the newspaper every day, how many people out of 500 would be expected to read one every day?

____________________

____________________

STOP

Name ______________________________ Date ______________

# WORKING WITH GEOMETRY

**Directions: Darken the circle for the correct answer, or write in your answer.**

| **Try This** | Use the objects shown to help you answer each question. Remember that circumference and perimeter are the measurements around the outside of a figure, while area and volume are the measurements of the inside of a figure. |
|---|---|

**Sample A**

What is the volume of a packing box 10 inches long, 8 inches wide, and 12 inches high?

Ⓐ 30 in.$^3$ Ⓒ 920 in.$^3$

Ⓑ 80 in.$^3$ Ⓓ 960 in.$^3$

| **Think It Through** | The correct answer is D, 960 in.$^3$ To determine the volume of a rectangular prism, multiply length by width by height: $10 \times 8 \times 12 = 960$ in.$^3$ |
|---|---|

1. What is the area of the shaded portion of triangle ABC? (Use $A = \frac{1}{2}bh$.)

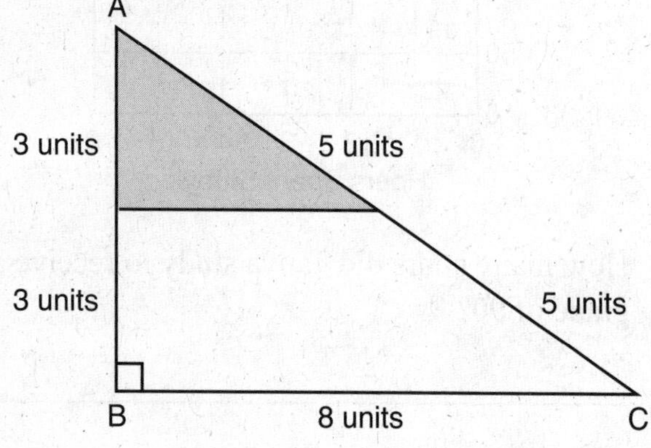


Ⓐ 6 square units

Ⓑ 8 square units

Ⓒ 12 square units

Ⓓ 24 square units

2. Which three-dimensional figure has exactly five faces?

Ⓕ cube

Ⓖ triangular prism

Ⓗ rectangular prism

Ⓙ cylinder

3. The new conference table is shown here. What is the approximate area of the table? (Use $A = \pi r^2$ and $\pi = 3.14$.)

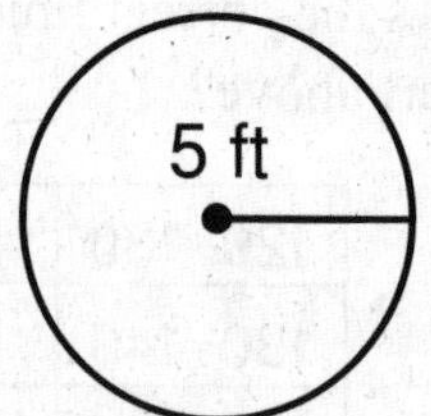


Ⓐ 78.5 sq ft

Ⓑ 49.29 sq ft

Ⓒ 34.85 sq ft

Ⓓ 15.7 sq ft

4. A sandbox measures 8 centimeters by 5 centimeters by 10 centimeters. How much sand is required to fill the box?

______________________________

______________________________

______________________________

GO ON

Name ______________________________ Date ______________

**5.** The diameter of circle $X$ is represented by which line segment?

Ⓕ $\overline{AX}$

Ⓖ $\overline{BX}$

Ⓗ $\overline{AB}$

Ⓙ $\overline{AC}$

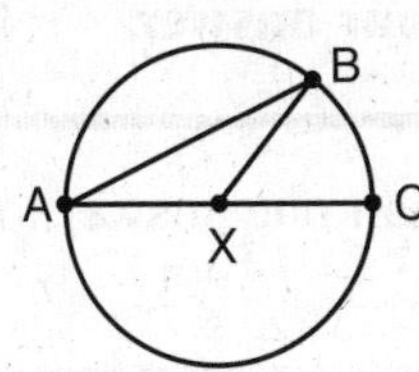


**6.** Which coordinates best represent the last point needed to complete the vertices of a rectangle?

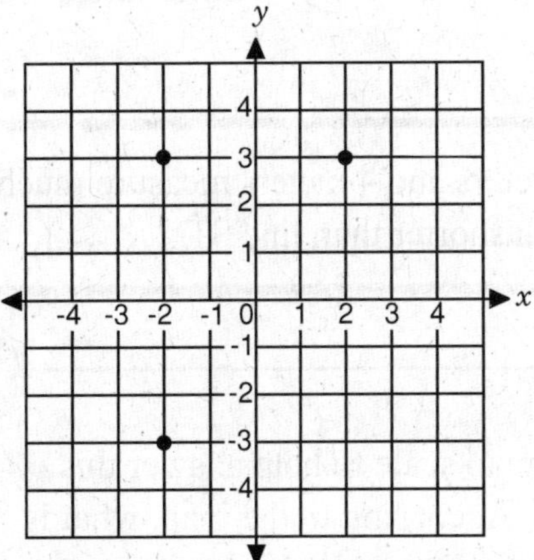

Ⓐ (−2, −2)

Ⓑ (2, −3)

Ⓒ (−2, 2)

Ⓓ (2, 2)

**7.** Which of these figures shows line $m$ perpendicular to line $n$?

Ⓕ 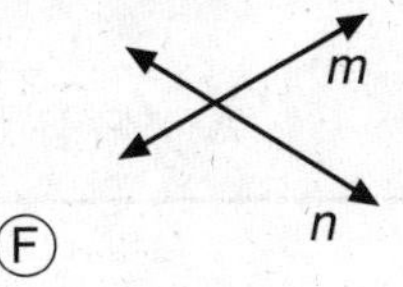


Ⓗ 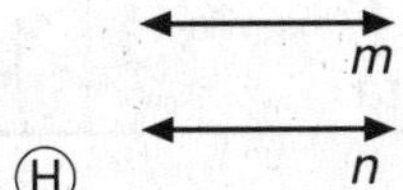


Ⓖ 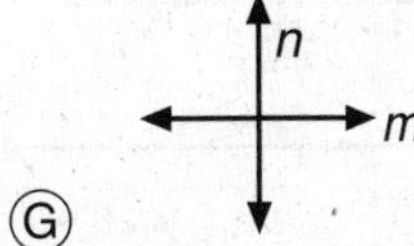


Ⓙ 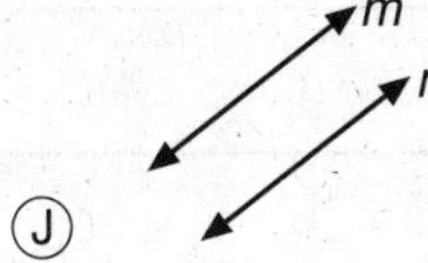


**8.** The light figure shows where the dark figure will be after it slides the direction shown by the arrow.

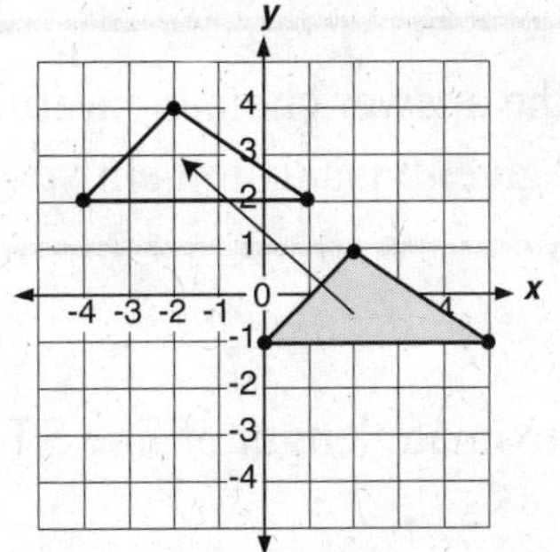

Which of the following shows the same slide?

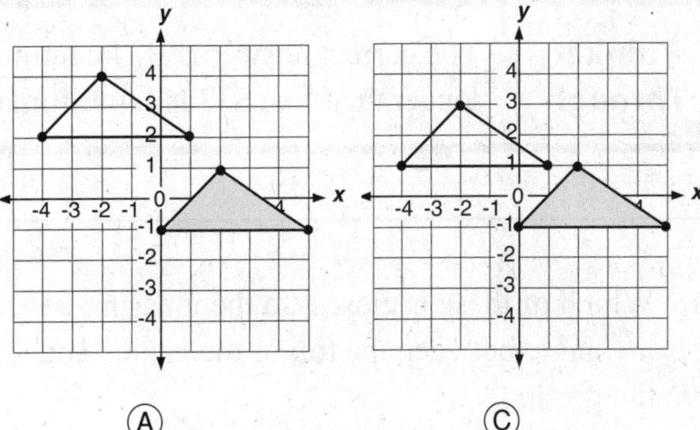

Ⓐ Ⓒ

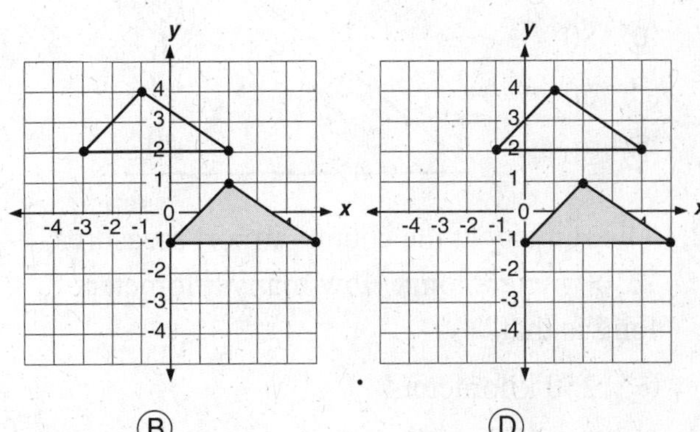

Ⓑ Ⓓ

**9.** A stone sundial has a diameter of 30 inches. What is the approximate circumference of the sundial? (Use $C = 2\pi r$ and $\pi = 3.14$.)

______________________________

______________________________

STOP

Name ______________________________ Date ______________

## USING MEASUREMENT

**Directions: Darken the circle for the correct answer, or write in your answer.**

| **Try This** | Study all the answer choices carefully. Sometimes more than one answer looks correct. Study any given visuals to help you choose your answer. |
|---|---|

**Sample A**

What is the approximate length of line ST shown here?

S•————————•T

Ⓐ 4 meters
Ⓑ 4 centimeters
Ⓒ 4 kilometers
Ⓓ 4 millimeters

| **Think It Through** | The correct answer is B, 4 centimeters. Both 4 kilometers and 4 meters measure much longer than line ST, and 4 millimeters measures much shorter than line ST. |
|---|---|

**1.** Which of these is closest to the measure of the angle between the top of the cactus and the ground?

Ⓐ 90°
Ⓑ 80°
Ⓒ 50°
Ⓓ 30°

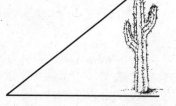

**2.** The runway at the county airport measures 2,300 meters long. How many kilometers long is that?

Ⓕ 230 kilometers
Ⓖ 23 kilometers
Ⓗ 2.3 kilometers
Ⓙ 0.23 kilometers

**3.** Use the map scale to help answer this question. According to the map, what is the shortest distance by railroad from Faramin to Oakton?

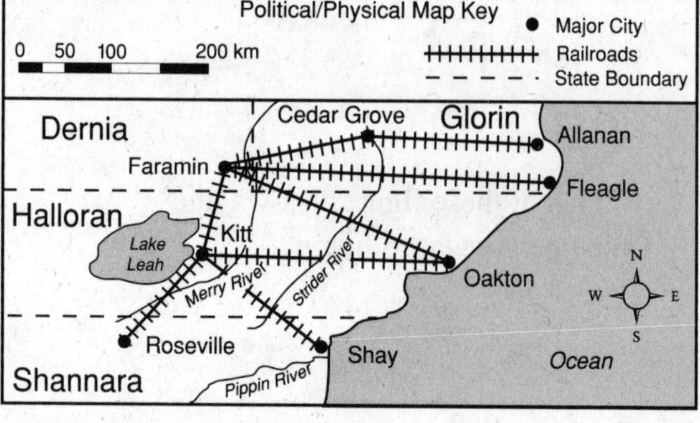


______________________________

______________________________

STOP

Name ______________________________ Date ______________

## ESTIMATING

**Directions: Darken the circle for the correct answer.**

| **Try This** | Round numbers when you estimate. For some problems, there are no exact answers. Then you should take your best guess. You can check your answer by using the numbers given in the problem. |
|---|---|

**Sample A**

Mrs. Rubin's garden store had 527 rosebushes. She sold 215 of them. Which is the best estimate of the number of rosebushes she has left?

Ⓐ 400
Ⓑ 300
Ⓒ 200
Ⓓ 100

| **Think It Through** | The correct answer is B. Start by rounding 527 rosebushes to 500. Then round 215 to 200. You couldn't have 400, 200, or 100 left. Check by subtracting 200 from 500. The best estimate is 300. |
|---|---|

**1.** Akiko bought $5\frac{2}{3}$ yards of imported silk at \$7.98 yard. She plans to use $3\frac{1}{2}$ yards of the silk to make a dress. About how much material will Akiko have left?

Ⓐ $1\frac{5}{8}$ yards
Ⓑ 2 yards
Ⓒ 3 yards
Ⓓ $3\frac{1}{2}$ yards

**2.** Martina bought craft supplies that totaled \$47.58. If the sales tax is 8%, which is the best estimate of the tax Martina paid?

Ⓕ \$3.00
Ⓖ \$4.00
Ⓗ \$9.89
Ⓙ \$15.78

**3.** A sculptor makes a scale drawing of a statue he is sculpting. If he wants the statue to be 50 feet tall, which is a reasonable scale for his drawing?

Ⓐ 1 inch represents 1 foot
Ⓑ $\frac{3}{4}$ inch represents 1 foot
Ⓒ inch represents 1 foot
Ⓓ inch represents 1 foot

**4.** Benjamin started with 3.18 kilograms of flour. He used 664 grams to make a cake. What is the best estimate of the amount of flour he has left?

Ⓕ 1,000 grams
Ⓖ 1,500 grams
Ⓗ 2,300 grams
Ⓙ 4,000 grams

**5.** A baby-sitting service charges \$1.75 per child per hour. *About* how much would a family pay the service to baby-sit 3 of their children for 6 hours?

Ⓐ \$9.50
Ⓑ \$12.00
Ⓒ \$18.00
Ⓓ \$36.00

**6.** The scale on a map of New Jersey shows that 4 inches equals 25 miles. The distance from Newark to Atlantic City measures 14.2 inches on the map. *About* how many miles does that represent?

Ⓕ less than 40 miles
Ⓖ between 80 and 90 miles
Ⓗ between 100 and 110 miles
Ⓙ more than 115 miles

STOP

Name ______________________________ Date ______________

# USING PROBLEM-SOLVING STRATEGIES

**Directions: Darken the circle for the correct answer, or write in your answer.**

| **Try This** | Study the words in each problem carefully. Then decide what you have to do to find the answer. |
|---|---|

**Sample A**

Lina makes decorative pillows. She can sew a pillow in 25 minutes. What additional information is needed to find how long it takes Lina to sew an entire set of pillows?

Ⓐ the length of each pillow

Ⓑ the weight of each pillow

Ⓒ the cost of the materials

Ⓓ the number of pillows in a set

| **Think It Through** | The correct answer is D. You do not need to know the length or weight of each pillow, nor the cost of the materials. To find out how long it takes to make a *set,* you need to know the number of pillows in a set. |
|---|---|

1. How many non-straight angles can you find in this figure?

Ⓐ 6
Ⓑ 10
Ⓒ 15
Ⓓ 18

2. All of Sam's friends like to play chess. Some of his friends like to play checkers. None of Sam's friends likes to play bridge. Perry, who is the school chess champion, also likes to play bridge. Which of the following statements must be true?

Ⓕ Sam and Perry are friends.
Ⓖ Perry plays checkers.
Ⓗ Sam plays bridge.
Ⓙ Sam and Perry are not friends.

3. What can be done to Side A to balance the scale? Each cube equals $1\frac{1}{2}$ cylinders.

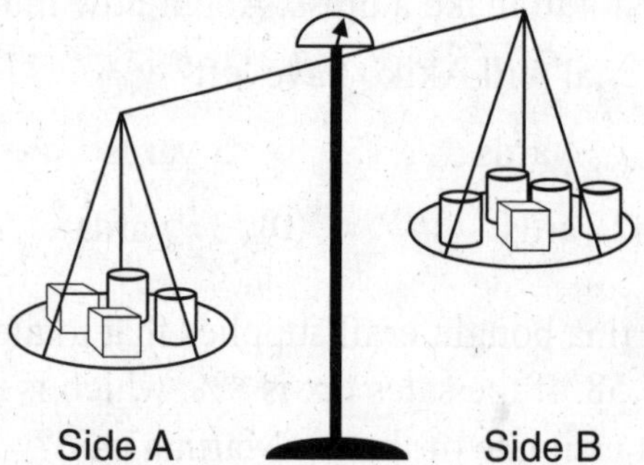


Ⓐ Remove one cube and add one cylinder.
Ⓑ Remove one cylinder and add one cube.
Ⓒ Add two cylinders.
Ⓓ Remove two cylinders and add one cube.

4. Chuck's birthday is 2 days before Linus's. Lucy's birthday is 3 days after Marcy's. Patty's birthday is 4 days before Lucy's. If Marcy's birthday is March 10, when is Patty's birthday?

______________________________

GO ON

Name ________________________________________ Date ____________________

5. The sum of the first and last numbers in Max's apartment number is twice the sum of the last two numbers. Which of these could be Max's apartment number?

Ⓕ 842

Ⓖ 824

Ⓗ 428

Ⓙ 248

6. The price offered per pound for cattle was \$7.89. The first cow weighed 1,289.6 pounds, the second cow weighed 1,065.2 pounds, and the third weighed 1,134.07 pounds. Which of these questions <u>cannot</u> be answered using the information given?

Ⓐ What is the total weight of the cattle?

Ⓑ How much weight did the heaviest cow gain in one year?

Ⓒ How much weight difference is there between the lightest and the heaviest cow?

Ⓓ What is the total price paid for the 2 heaviest cows?

7. There are 13 students in one lunch line and 29 students in the other lunch line. How many students would need to move from the long line to the short line to make both lines equal?

_______________________________________

_______________________________________

8. There were 72 children at the picnic. If they were organized into 6 even softball teams, how many children were on each team?

_______________________________________

_______________________________________

**Use the picture shown here to answer questions 9 and 10.**

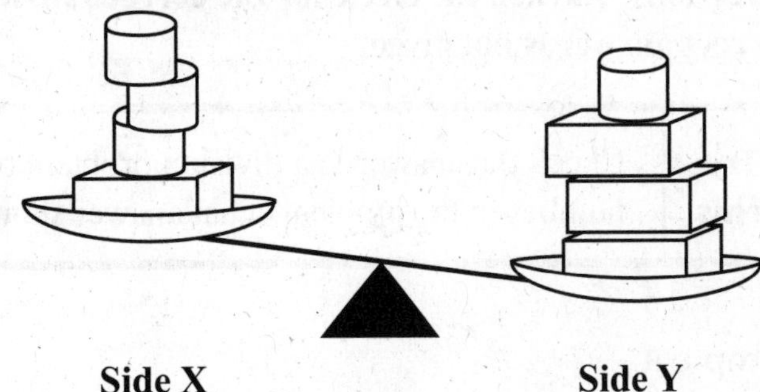


9. If 1 cylinder equaled 3 rectangular prisms, which of the following would be true?

Ⓕ Side X > Side Y

Ⓖ Side X < Side Y

Ⓗ Side X = Side Y

Ⓙ Side X ≈ Side Y

10. If each rectangular prism is equal to 2 cylinders, what should be added to Side X so that the scales balance?

Ⓐ 2 rectangular prisms

Ⓑ 1 rectangular prism and 1 cylinder

Ⓒ 2 cylinders

Ⓓ 1 cylinder

11. Alexa bought a beach towel for \$11, a beach umbrella for \$12, and sunscreen for \$7. She paid for the items with a \$50 bill. What information is <u>not</u> needed to find out how much Alexa paid for her purchases?

Ⓕ The beach towel costs \$11.

Ⓖ The beach umbrella costs \$12.

Ⓗ The sunscreen costs \$7.

Ⓙ She paid with a \$50 bill.

STOP

Name ______________________ Date ______________

# USING COMPUTATION

**Directions: Darken the circle for the correct answer. Darken the circle for *NH, Not Here*, if the correct answer is not given.**

| **Try This** | Check the answer to a division problem by multiplying. Multiply the answer by the smaller number in the problem. That answer should equal the larger number in the problem. |
|---|---|

**Sample A**

$1{,}440 \div 12 =$

- Ⓐ 112
- Ⓑ 102
- Ⓒ 144
- Ⓓ 120
- Ⓔ NH

| **Think It Through** | The correct answer is D, 120. Check this by multiplying. Since $120 \times 12 = 1{,}440$, you know the answer is correct. |
|---|---|

STOP

**1.** $8 \times \frac{3}{4} =$

- Ⓐ $8\frac{3}{4}$
- Ⓑ 6
- Ⓒ 5
- Ⓓ $\frac{3}{4}$
- Ⓔ NH

**2.** $2\frac{5}{12} + \frac{6}{12} =$

- Ⓕ $2\frac{11}{24}$
- Ⓖ $2\frac{1}{12}$
- Ⓗ $2\frac{11}{12}$
- Ⓙ $2\frac{1}{2}$
- Ⓚ NH

**3.** $0.28 \times 0.06 =$

- Ⓐ 0.0168
- Ⓑ 0.168
- Ⓒ 1.68
- Ⓓ 1.168
- Ⓔ NH

**4.** $24.73 + 0.098 =$

- Ⓕ 24.728
- Ⓖ 2.571
- Ⓗ 0.02571
- Ⓙ 25.71
- Ⓚ NH

**5.** $4 \div \frac{3}{5} =$

- Ⓐ $\frac{3}{20}$
- Ⓑ $\frac{5}{12}$
- Ⓒ $6\frac{2}{3}$
- Ⓓ $2\frac{2}{5}$
- Ⓔ NH

**6.** $-2 \times -9 =$

- Ⓕ −18
- Ⓖ −11
- Ⓗ −7
- Ⓙ 18
- Ⓚ NH

STOP

Name ____________________ Date ____________________

# USING COMPUTATION IN CONTEXT

**Directions: Darken the circle for the correct answer. Darken the circle in context for *NH, Not Here*, if the correct answer is not given, or write in the answer.**

| **Try This** | Read the word problem carefully. Then set up the word problem as a numerical formula. Solve the formula, and compare your answer with the answer choices. |
|---|---|

**Sample A**

A bookcase has 4 shelves and contains 168 books. If the books are evenly divided on the shelves, how many books are there on each shelf?

Ⓐ 40
Ⓑ 172
Ⓒ 164
Ⓓ 42
Ⓔ NH

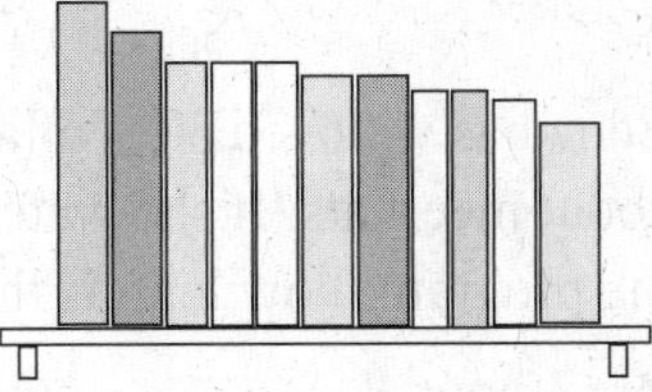

| **Think It Through** | To find how many books are on one shelf, divide the number of books by the number of shelves. Since 168 ÷ 4 = <u>42</u>, the answer is <u>D</u>. |
|---|---|

1. Mariah spent half of her allowance for a gift. She then deposited \$4.50 into her savings account and spent the remaining \$6.00 bowling. What percent of her allowance did Mariah put into savings?

Ⓐ 21.4%
Ⓑ 28.5%
Ⓒ 50%
Ⓓ 78.5%
Ⓔ NH

2. The Canoe Club took 72 adults and 12 students on a trip. Each bus held 24 people. How many buses were there?

____________________

____________________

3. The Fox family is driving 1,500 miles. They drove 475 miles yesterday and 520 miles today. How many more miles will they drive?

Ⓐ 995 miles
Ⓑ 505 miles
Ⓒ 2,495 miles
Ⓓ 45 miles
Ⓔ NH

4. If Esteban swims the same distance every day, and he swims $10\frac{1}{2}$ miles in two weeks, how many miles does he swim each day?

Ⓕ $1\frac{1}{4}$ miles
Ⓖ $\frac{7}{8}$ mile
Ⓗ $\frac{3}{4}$ mile
Ⓙ $\frac{2}{3}$ mile
Ⓚ NH

GO ON

Name ______________________________ Date ______________

**5.** Maurice made $4\frac{1}{2}$ quarts of gumbo. If one serving is $\frac{1}{4}$ quart, how many servings did Maurice make?

Ⓕ 18

Ⓖ 12

Ⓗ 9

Ⓙ $5\frac{1}{2}$

Ⓚ NH

**6.** Edna has watched 30% of a documentary about meerkats. If she watched 36 minutes of the program, how long is the documentary?

Ⓐ 1 hour

Ⓑ $1\frac{1}{2}$ hours

Ⓒ $2\frac{1}{2}$ hours

Ⓓ 3 hours

Ⓔ NH

**7.** Yesterday it snowed 37.5% of the day. What is that percent rounded to the nearest compatible fraction?

Ⓕ $\frac{1}{2}$

Ⓖ $\frac{1}{3}$

Ⓗ $\frac{2}{5}$

Ⓙ $\frac{1}{4}$

Ⓚ $\frac{1}{37}$

**8.** After the party, there were $1\frac{1}{2}$ pepperoni pizzas, $\frac{5}{6}$ of a hamburger pizza, and $\frac{1}{3}$ of a cheese pizza left. What was the total amount of pizza left?

Ⓐ $\frac{11}{18}$

Ⓑ $2\frac{1}{6}$

Ⓒ $2\frac{2}{3}$

Ⓓ $3\frac{1}{6}$

Ⓔ $3\frac{1}{2}$

**9.** The Severn suspension bridge in England is 987.8568 meters long. What is its length rounded to the nearest thousandth?

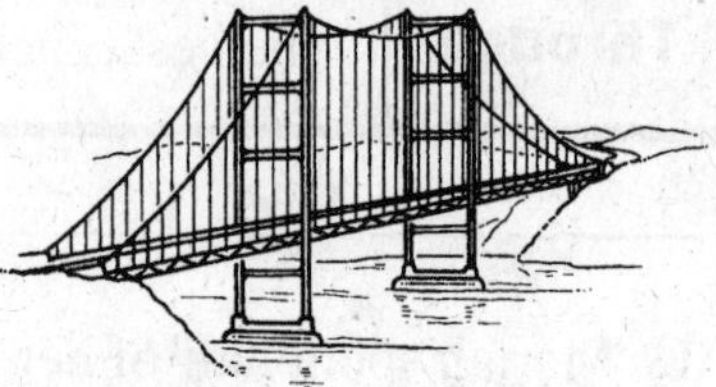

Ⓕ 987.857

Ⓖ 987.9

Ⓗ 987.856

Ⓙ 988

Ⓚ 988.900

**10.** Darcy earns $4.55 an hour working at the theater in the mall. How much does she make if she works 14 hours this weekend?

______________________________

______________________________

STOP

Name ______________________ Date ______________

# TEST 1: MATH PROBLEM SOLVING

**Sample A**

Which fraction is smallest in value?

Ⓐ $\frac{3}{8}$

Ⓑ $\frac{3}{10}$

Ⓒ $\frac{7}{10}$

Ⓓ $\frac{1}{2}$

**For questions 1–45, darken the circle for the correct answer, or write in your answer.**

1. Light travels at a speed of 186,282 miles per second. How could this distance be expressed using scientific notation?

   Ⓐ $1{,}862.82 \times 10^3$

   Ⓑ $186.282 \times 10^{-3}$

   Ⓒ $1.86282 \times 10^4$

   Ⓓ $1.86282 \times 10^5$

2. Which point best represents 7.8 on the number line?

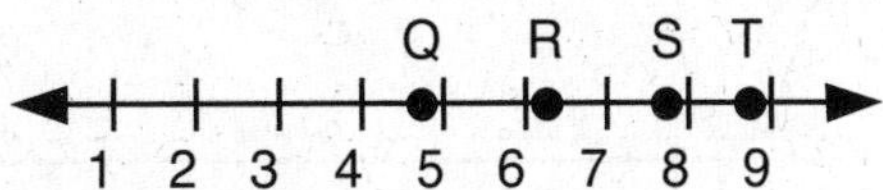


   Ⓕ Q

   Ⓖ R

   Ⓗ S

   Ⓙ T

3. Which is not a way to write $\frac{3}{4}$?

   Ⓐ 0.75%

   Ⓑ 0.75

   Ⓒ $\frac{75}{100}$

   Ⓓ 75%

4. What is the value of the 4 in the number 872.0654?

   Ⓕ 4 tenths

   Ⓖ 4 hundredths

   Ⓗ 4 ten-thousandths

   Ⓙ 4 hundred-thousandths

5. Which decimal shows the part of the figure that is shaded?

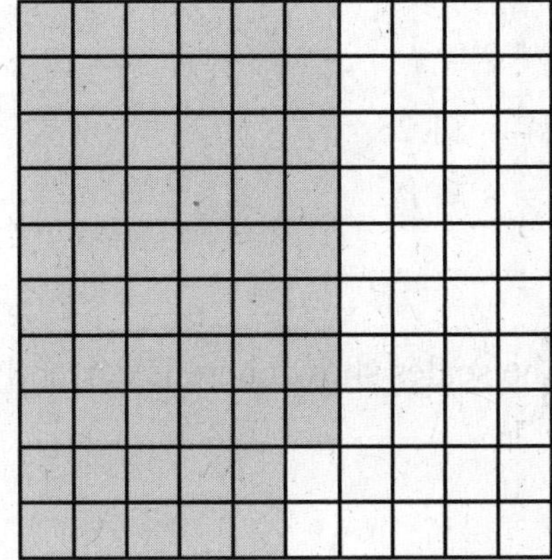

   Ⓐ 00.58 Ⓒ 5.8

   Ⓑ 0.58 Ⓓ 5.80

6. Which of the following numbers is greater than −1?

   Ⓕ 0 Ⓗ −3

   Ⓖ −2 Ⓙ −4

7. Which fraction is equivalent to $\frac{6}{9}$?

   Ⓐ $\frac{2}{3}$ Ⓒ $\frac{3}{9}$

   Ⓑ $\frac{3}{6}$ Ⓓ $\frac{4}{8}$

8. Which number listed here is not a prime number?

   Ⓕ 9 Ⓗ 7

   Ⓖ 11 Ⓙ 5

GO ON

Name ______________________________ Date ________________

**9.** The mystery number $M$ is 5 more than twice the value of 12. Which number sentence could be used to find the value of $M$?

Ⓐ $M = (12 \div 2) - 5$

Ⓑ $M = (12 \times 2) + 5$

Ⓒ $M = 12 + (2 \times 5)$

Ⓓ $M = 5 + 2 + 12$

**10.** Lena bought 8 ounces of walnuts. If the walnuts sell for \$1.25 a pound, which number sentence could be used to find $P$, the price Lena paid for the walnuts?

Ⓕ $\$1.25 \div 2 = P$

Ⓖ $(8 + 8) \times \$1.25 = P$

Ⓗ $\$1.25 \div 8 = P$

Ⓙ $(\$1.25 \div 2) \times 8 = P$

**11.** Which of the scales shown here is correctly balanced?

Ⓐ 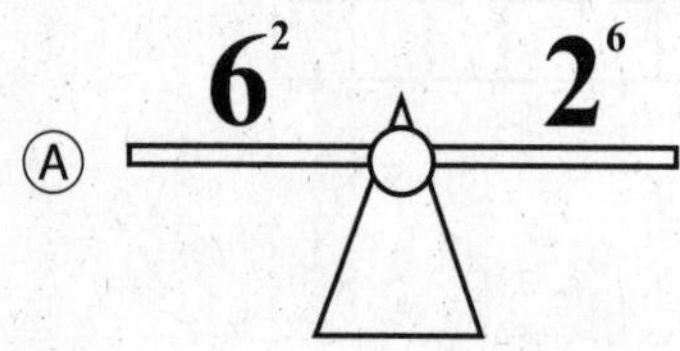


Ⓑ 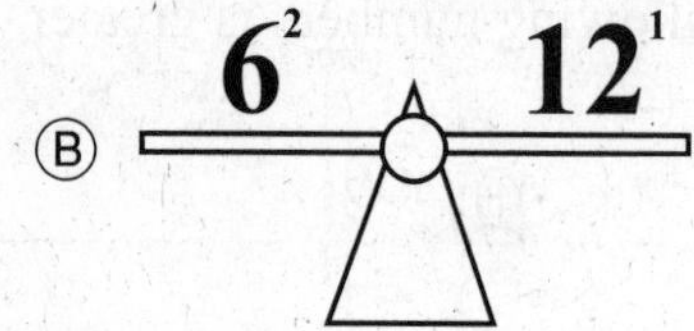


Ⓒ 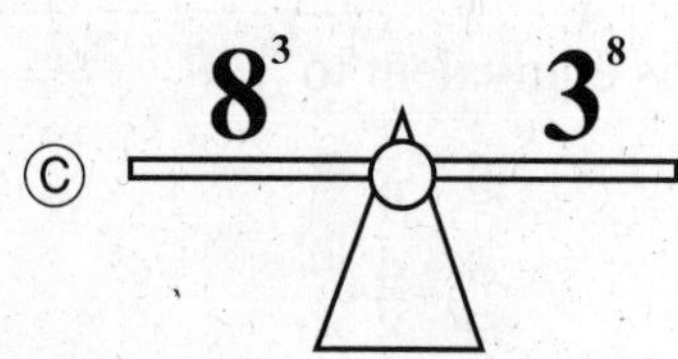


Ⓓ 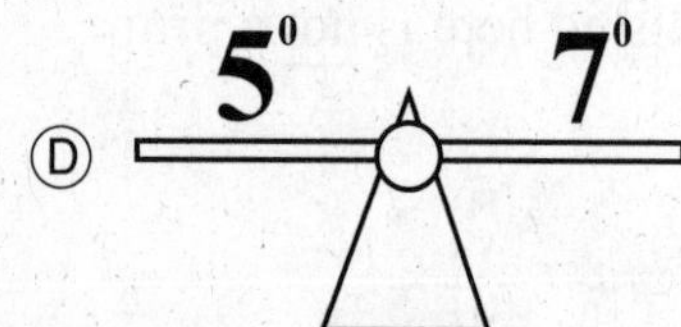


**12.** Which expression demonstrates that 8 multiplied by $y$ equals 120?

Ⓕ $\frac{8}{y} = 120$

Ⓖ $120 \times 8 = y$

Ⓗ $8y = 120$

Ⓙ $120 > \frac{y}{8}$

**13.** Choose the symbol that makes this statement true. $7\frac{7}{12}$ ______ $7\frac{5}{11}$

Ⓐ $\geq$

Ⓑ $<$

Ⓒ $=$

Ⓓ $>$

**14.** Which expression means the same as $15 \times n - 2$?

Ⓕ $15n - 2$

Ⓖ $15(n - 2)$

Ⓗ $15 - n - 2$

Ⓙ $13n$

**15.** For every pound Miguel lifts in a weight-lifting contest, his sponsor will contribute \$3 to Miguel's college savings. If Miguel lifts 350 pounds, how much will his sponsor contribute?

______________________________

______________________________

**16.** There is one ripe tomato in a garden on the first day. The number of ripe tomatoes in the garden increases by three each day. If this pattern continues, how many ripe tomatoes would be produced on the fifteenth day?

______________________________

______________________________

GO ON

Name ____________________ Date ____________

**17.** It is Celina's turn in a board game she is playing with her friends. What is the probability that Celina will lose a turn on this spin?

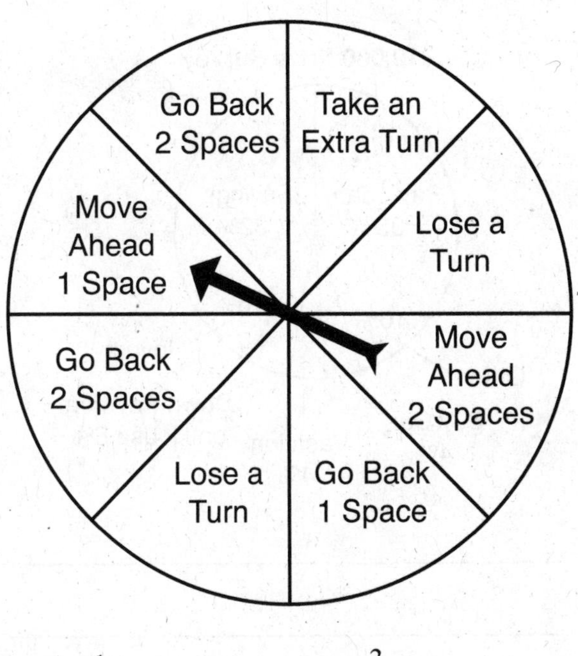


Ⓐ $\frac{1}{8}$ Ⓒ $\frac{3}{8}$

Ⓑ $\frac{1}{4}$ Ⓓ $\frac{5}{8}$

**18.** How many beverage-and-dessert combinations could possibly be ordered at Malcolm's Coffee Shop?

**Malcolm's Coffee Shop**

| Drinks | | Desserts | |
|---|---|---|---|
| Coffee | \$0.85 | Cake | \$1.85 |
| Milk | \$0.55 | Cheesecake | \$1.45 |
| Orange Juice | \$0.65 | Donuts | \$0.95 |

Ⓕ 3 Ⓗ 9

Ⓖ 6 Ⓙ 12

**19.** A special machine multiplies any number entered into it by 9. The table shows how numbers are changed. Which numbers complete the table? Write them in the empty boxes.

| **Original number** | 4 | 6 | 9 |
|---|---|---|---|
| **New Number** | 36 | | |

**20.** This graph shows the number of students who walked to school during a certain week. What is the average (mean) number of students who walked to school during this week?

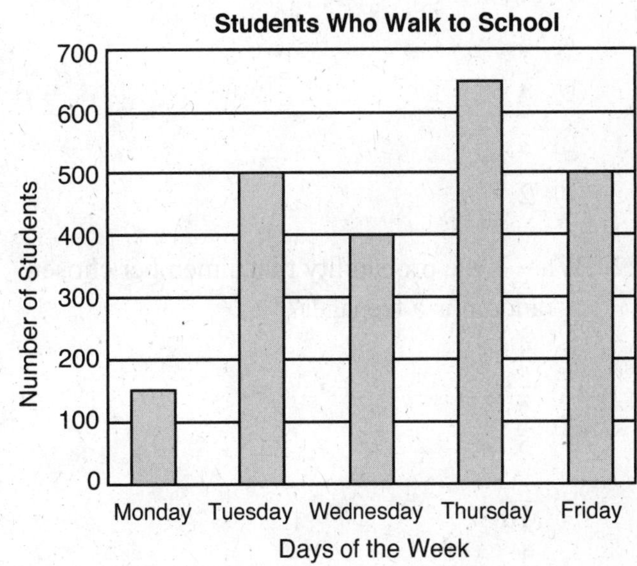


______________________________

______________________________

GO ON

Name ______________________ Date ______________

**The stem-and-leaf chart below shows the ages of members of a hiking club. Use the chart to answer questions 21 through 23.**

| Mountain Hiking Club | |
|---|---|
| **Stem** | **Leaf** |
| 1 | 7, 7, 8, 9 |
| 2 | 1, 2, 2, 2, 4 |
| 3 | 0, 3, 3, 5 |
| 4 | 1, 1, 4, 5, 7 |
| 5 | 0, 3 |

**21.** How many 22-year-olds are members of the hiking club?

Ⓐ 5

Ⓑ 4

Ⓒ 3

Ⓓ 2

**22.** What is the probability that a member chosen at random is a teenager?

Ⓕ $\frac{4}{5}$

Ⓖ $\frac{2}{5}$

Ⓗ $\frac{3}{10}$

Ⓙ $\frac{1}{5}$

**23.** If one of the members made a tally chart showing the number of members in each category, how many tally marks would be in the 30 – 40 row?

Ⓐ 4

Ⓑ 5

Ⓒ 8

Ⓓ 9

**24.** The graph shows 500 responses to the question, "How would you spend a prize of $10,000?" How many of the 500 would use the prize money as a down payment on a house?

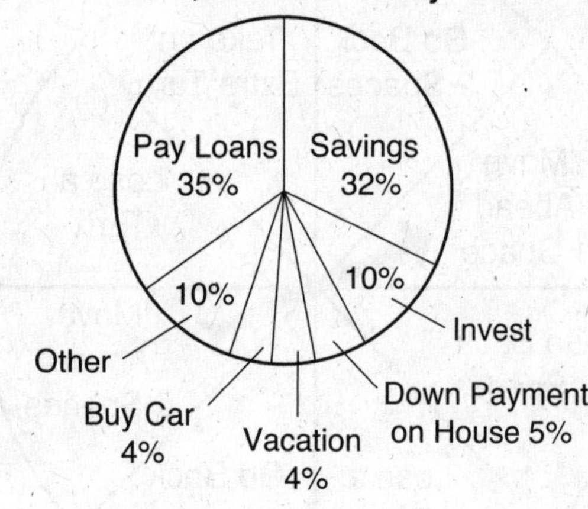


______________________________

______________________________

**Use the graph below to answer questions 25 and 26.**

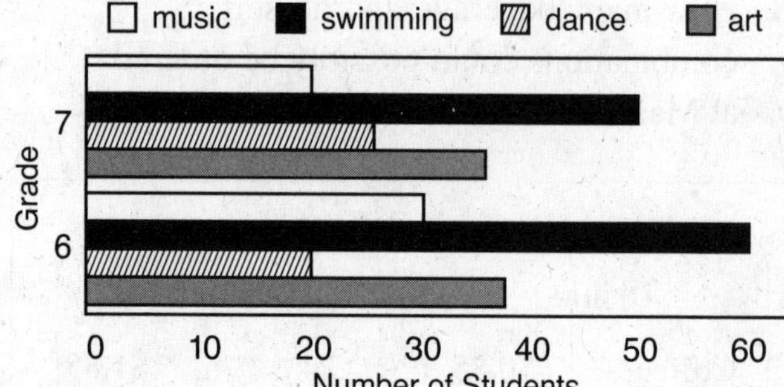


**25.** About what percent of students in Grade 7 play music after school?

Ⓕ 60% Ⓗ 30%

Ⓖ 45% Ⓙ 15%

**26.** About what percent of students in Grade 6 swim after school?

Ⓐ 20% Ⓒ 60%

Ⓑ 40% Ⓓ 100%

GO ON

Name ________________________________ Date ________________

27. Which transformation moves the figure from position A to position B?

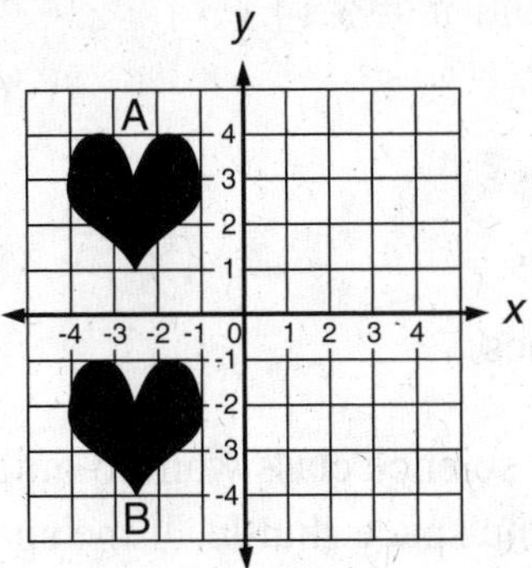


Ⓕ extension

Ⓖ rotation

Ⓗ reflection

Ⓙ translation

28. Which coordinates best represent the last point needed to complete the vertices of a trapezoid?

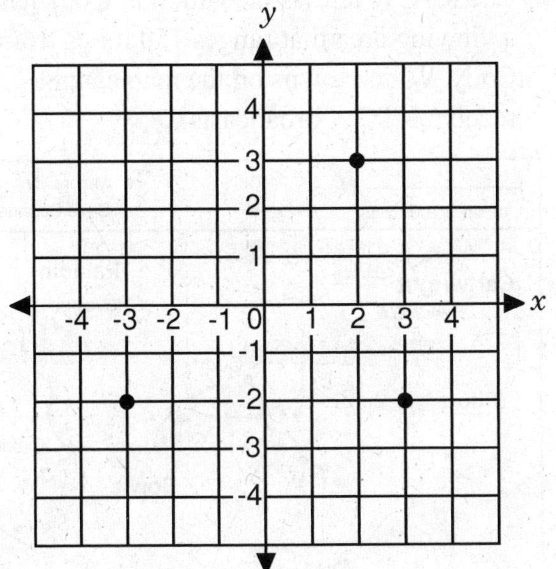


Ⓐ $(-2, -3)$

Ⓑ $(-2, -2)$

Ⓒ $(-2, 3)$

Ⓓ $(3, -3)$

29. How many faces does this figure have?

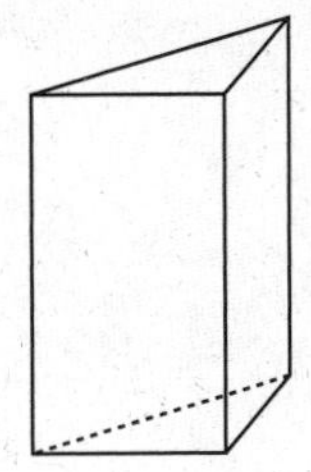

______________________________

______________________________

30. Pam's mother stores buttons in this wood box. What is the volume of the box?

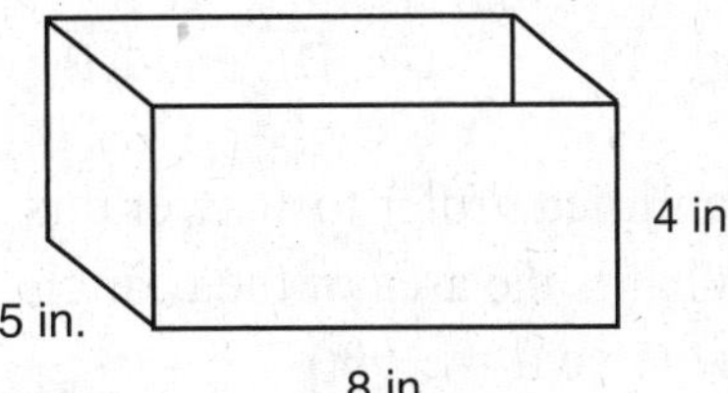


______________________________

______________________________

**A student wanted to see if the hours spent watching television relate to scores on a test.**

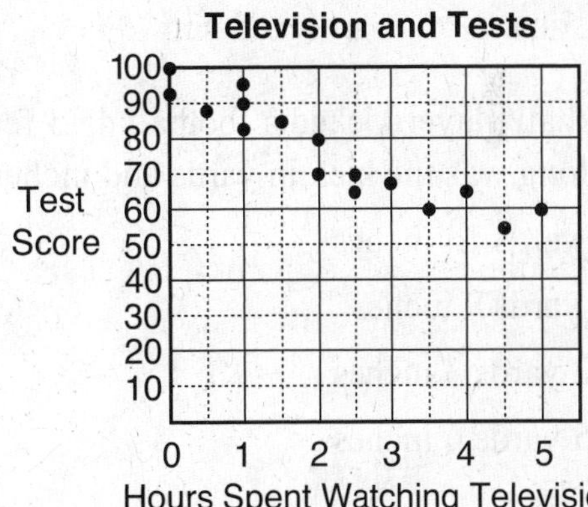


31. A student wanted to see if the hours spent watching television relate to scores on a test. According to the graph, 2 students watched 2 hours of television. What was their average score?

Ⓕ 80

Ⓖ 75

Ⓗ 70

Ⓙ 65

GO ON

Name ______________________________ Date ______________

**32.** Which 2 line segments are parallel in the figure shown here?

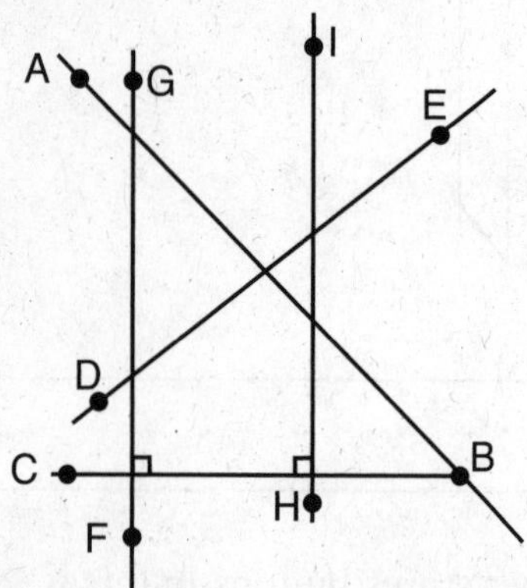


Ⓐ $\overline{FG}$ and $\overline{HI}$  Ⓒ $\overline{DE}$ and $\overline{CB}$

Ⓑ $\overline{CB}$ and $\overline{FG}$  Ⓓ $\overline{DE}$ and $\overline{AB}$

**33.** Use your centimeter ruler to answer this question. What is the area of the triangle shown here? (Use $A = \frac{1}{2}bh$.)

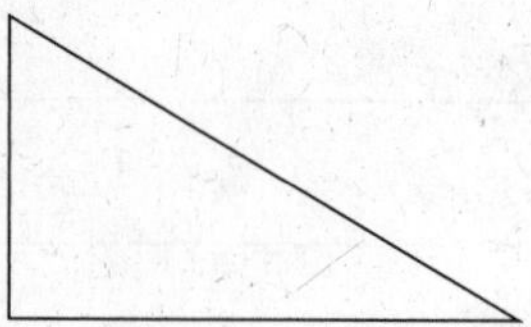

Ⓕ 3 $cm^2$  Ⓗ 4.5 $cm^2$

Ⓖ 3.5 $cm^2$  Ⓙ 5 $cm^2$

**34.** A football player kicked a football 45.5 feet. How long was the kick in yards and inches?

Ⓐ 2 yards 13 inches

Ⓑ 3 yards 9 inches

Ⓒ 12 yards 3 inches

Ⓓ 15 yards 6 inches

**35.** What is the diameter of the circle shown here?

Ⓕ 2 inches

Ⓖ 3 inches

Ⓗ 10 inches

Ⓙ 12 inches

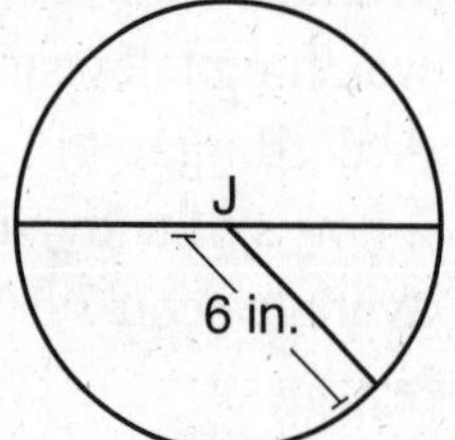


**36.** The diameter of a pizza is 14 inches. What is the circumference?
(Use $C \times 2\pi r$ and $\pi = 3.14$.)

Ⓐ 10.99 inches

Ⓑ 21.98 inches

Ⓒ 43.96 inches

Ⓓ 307.72 inches

**37.** Members of the science class want to build a scale model of the space shuttle. If the space shuttle is approximately 122 feet in length, 57 feet high, and has a wingspan of 78 feet, which is a reasonable scale for the model?

Ⓕ 1 inch represents 20 feet

Ⓖ 1 inch represents 100 feet

Ⓗ $\frac{1}{2}$ inch represents 1 foot

Ⓙ $\frac{1}{2}$ inch represents 100 feet

**38.** The KTCW television station in Cody has a viewing area that ranges 150 miles from Cody. Which towns on the map cannot receive KTCW broadcasts?

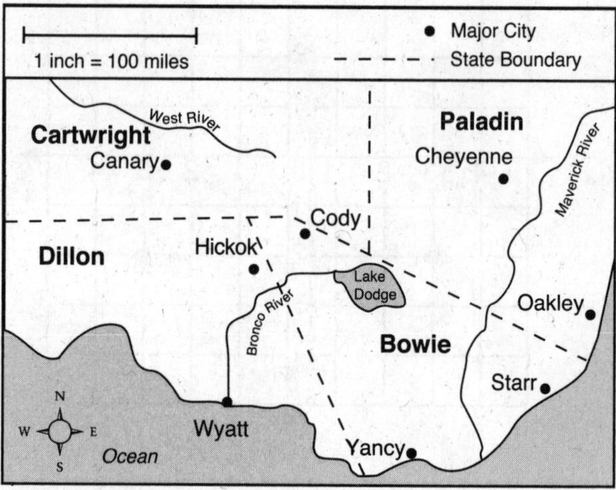


________________________________________

________________________________________

________________________________________

________________________________________

GO ON

Name ______________________________ Date ______________

**39.** Kyle has earned 40% of the money he needs to buy a used car. If the selling price of the car is $7,850, *about* how much more money does Kyle need to buy the car?

Ⓐ $2,500

Ⓑ $3,000

Ⓒ $4,000

Ⓓ $5,000

**40.** East Willow Town was founded in 1875. The population has grown over the years. What information is not needed to find out how much the population has grown?

Ⓕ the population in 1875

Ⓖ how many babies have been born in East Willow Town

Ⓗ how many people have moved to East Willow Town

Ⓙ how many towns have been founded in the state

**41.** Each cone weighs 2 kilograms. What is the weight of 1 cube?

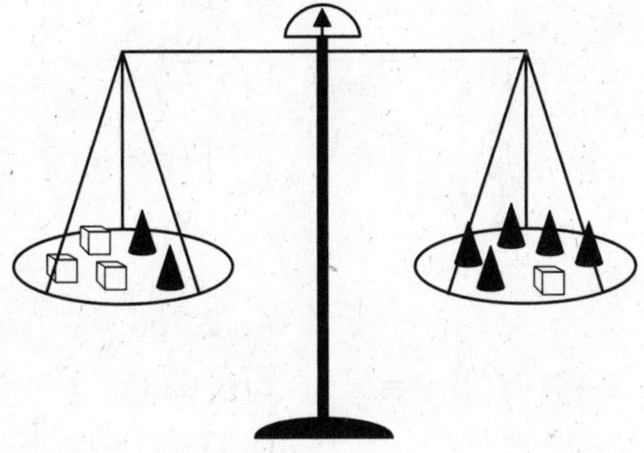

Ⓐ 1.5 kilograms

Ⓑ 2 kilograms

Ⓒ 3 kilograms

Ⓓ 3.5 kilograms

**42.** Allen drank $\frac{2}{3}$ of a pint of water in the morning, $1\frac{1}{4}$ pints in the afternoon, and $1\frac{1}{3}$ pints in the evening. Which is closest to the total amount of water Allen drank?

Ⓕ 14 ounces

Ⓖ 6 cups

Ⓗ $3\frac{1}{2}$ quarts

Ⓙ 1 gallon

**43.** Chris is older than his brother Sam. Ralph is older than Sam, but younger than Chris. Sam is also younger than Ben. Chris is not the oldest. What is the correct order of the brothers from youngest to oldest?

Ⓐ Sam, Ralph, Chris, Ben

Ⓑ Sam, Ben, Ralph, Chris

Ⓒ Sam, Chris, Ralph, Ben

Ⓓ Ben, Chris, Sam, Ralph

**44.** There were four cross-country team members running in an event. Robin finished after Earl. Nick finished after Robin. Neal finished ahead of Robin but after Earl. Which of the following shows the order in which the runners finished the event from first to last?

Ⓕ Earl, Neal, Robin, Nick

Ⓖ Neal, Earl, Robin, Nick

Ⓗ Robin, Earl, Nick, Neal

Ⓙ Nick, Robin, Neal, Earl

**45.** Candace collected the most money for the fund raiser. Randy collected $14 more than Gina, but $22 less than Candace. If Gina collected $98, then how much did Candace collect?

______________________________

______________________________

STOP

Name ______________________________ Date ______________

# TEST 2: MATH PROCEDURES

## Sample A

$120 \div 24 =$

Ⓐ 6
Ⓑ 5
Ⓒ 4
Ⓓ 50
Ⓔ NH

STOP

## Sample B

Socks are packed 5 pairs to a box and 9 boxes to a carton. How many pairs of socks are in a carton?

Ⓕ 4

Ⓖ 40
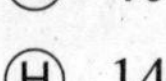
Ⓗ 14
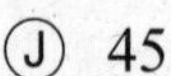
Ⓙ 45
Ⓚ NH

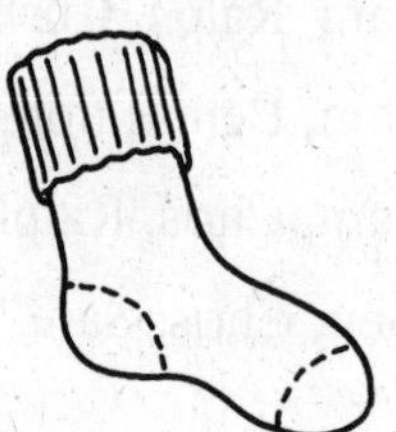

STOP

**For questions 1–14, darken the circle for the correct answer. Darken the circle for *NH*, *Not Here*, if the correct answer is not given. If there are no choices given, write in your answer.**

**1.** $0.872 - 0.681 =$

Ⓐ 0.191
Ⓑ 0.211
Ⓒ 0.190
Ⓓ 1.552
Ⓔ NH

**2.** $12\frac{5}{7} - 5\frac{4}{7}$

Ⓕ $13\frac{1}{7}$
Ⓖ $7\frac{9}{7}$
Ⓗ $7\frac{1}{7}$
Ⓙ $8\frac{1}{7}$
Ⓚ NH

**3.** $8 + -7 =$

Ⓐ −15
Ⓑ 1
Ⓒ −1
Ⓓ 15
Ⓔ NH

**4.** $\frac{4}{7} \times \frac{3}{7} =$

Ⓕ $\frac{12}{49}$
Ⓖ $\frac{3}{4}$
Ⓗ $1\frac{1}{3}$
Ⓙ $\frac{7}{14}$
Ⓚ NH

**5.** $17.6 - 9.4 =$

Ⓐ 12.2
Ⓑ 8.10
Ⓒ 8.2
Ⓓ 9.2
Ⓔ NH

**6.** $7\frac{2}{3} + 10\frac{1}{4}$

Ⓕ $17\frac{10}{12}$
Ⓖ $18\frac{1}{2}$
Ⓗ $17\frac{3}{7}$
Ⓙ $17\frac{2}{12}$
Ⓚ NH

**7.** $2{,}481 \times 285 =$

Ⓐ 2,766
Ⓑ 707,085
Ⓒ 37,215
Ⓓ 703,485
Ⓔ NH

**8.** $\frac{3}{4} \div 6 =$

______________________________

______________________________

GO ON

Name ______________________________ Date ______________________

9. In Pine Valley there are 5,678 one-story houses and 3,456 two-story houses. How many more one-story than two-story houses are there?

Ⓕ 1,898
Ⓖ 2,456
Ⓗ 2,222
Ⓙ 2,134
Ⓚ NH

10. A map was drawn to the scale of 1 cm = 20 miles. If the distance between two cities is $6\frac{1}{2}$ cm, how many miles apart are the two cities?

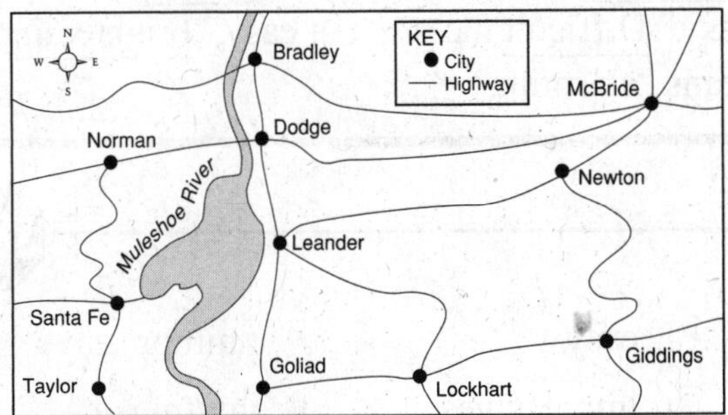


Ⓐ $26\frac{1}{2}$ miles
Ⓑ 120 miles
Ⓒ 130 miles
Ⓓ 18 miles
Ⓔ NH

11. Of the 48 students who signed up for a dance class, only $\frac{1}{2}$ had dance experience. During the first week, $\frac{1}{3}$ of the inexperienced students dropped the class. How many of the inexperienced students continued taking the dance class?

Ⓕ 8
Ⓖ 16
Ⓗ 24
Ⓙ 40
Ⓚ NH

12. Rita and Jack worked on a magazine article. As editor, Jack will receive 60% of the fee. Rita, as photographer, will receive 40% of the fee. If the total fee is $1,200, what will Rita be paid?

Ⓐ $900
Ⓑ $720
Ⓒ $540
Ⓓ $480
Ⓔ NH

13. Maria scored 19.2 points for her team in two field events—the high jump and the triple jump. She scored 9.4 points in the high jump. How many points did Maria score in the triple jump?

Ⓕ 9.8
Ⓖ 10.3
Ⓗ 0.9
Ⓙ 9.4
Ⓚ NH

14. Nicky recently won $12,567 in a raffle. What is that amount rounded to the nearest hundred?

______________________________

______________________________

STOP

Name ______________________________ Date ______________

# Unit 7: Listening 

## UNDERSTANDING WORD MEANINGS

**Directions: Darken the circle for the word or words that best complete the sentence you hear.**

| **Try This** | Listen carefully to the sentence. Then look at the answer choices. Decide which words you know are wrong. Then look at the remaining words to make your choice. |
|---|---|

**Sample A**

Ⓐ comforting
Ⓑ simple
Ⓒ difficult
Ⓓ frightening

| **Think It Through** | The correct answer is C. All of the answer choices are descriptions of something. Comforting means "soothing." Simple means "easy." Difficult means "not easy." Frightening means "alarming." |
|---|---|

STOP

**1.** Ⓐ an assistance Ⓒ a recovery
Ⓑ an obstacle Ⓓ an entertainment

**2.** Ⓕ unclear Ⓗ misleading
Ⓖ direct Ⓙ specific

**3.** Ⓐ gentle Ⓒ perturbed
Ⓑ hostile Ⓓ confused

**4.** Ⓕ description Ⓗ prescription
Ⓖ cause Ⓙ result

**5.** Ⓐ happy Ⓒ unhappy
Ⓑ disappointed Ⓓ depressed

**6.** Ⓕ easy Ⓗ unimpressive
Ⓖ impressive Ⓙ inviting

**7.** Ⓐ increased Ⓒ decreased
Ⓑ ended Ⓓ strengthened

**8.** Ⓕ assorted Ⓗ specific
Ⓖ similar Ⓙ unusual

**9.** Ⓐ stopped Ⓒ tripped
Ⓑ helped Ⓓ shoved

**10.** Ⓕ ancient Ⓗ false
Ⓖ valuable Ⓙ genuine

STOP

Name ______________________ Date ______________

## BUILDING LISTENING SKILLS 

**Directions: Darken the circle for the word or words that best answer the question.**

| **Try This** | Form a picture of the passage in your mind. Listen carefully for details given in the passage. |
|---|---|

**Sample A**

Ⓐ an advertisement
Ⓑ a gardening book
Ⓒ a novel
Ⓓ a fashion magazine

| **Think It Through** | The correct answer is B. This kind of information would most likely appear in a book about gardening. |
|---|---|

STOP

1. Ⓐ the dances that could be held there
   Ⓑ the new floor
   Ⓒ the equipment
   Ⓓ the pleasant environment

2. Ⓕ tests
   Ⓖ games
   Ⓗ dances
   Ⓙ assemblies

3. Ⓐ the school principal
   Ⓑ the person who donated money for the new gym
   Ⓒ a teacher
   Ⓓ the school basketball coach

4. Ⓕ in an encyclopedia
   Ⓖ in a magazine
   Ⓗ in a school newspaper
   Ⓙ in a textbook

5. Ⓐ please the Romans
   Ⓑ give athletes a chance to compete
   Ⓒ raise money for athletic clubs
   Ⓓ honor Greek gods and goddesses

6. Ⓕ in Rome
   Ⓖ in England
   Ⓗ in Greece
   Ⓙ in the United States

7. Ⓐ 400 years
   Ⓑ 1,500 years
   Ⓒ 100 years
   Ⓓ 1,200 years

8. Ⓕ 1777
   Ⓖ 1896
   Ⓗ 1900
   Ⓙ 1929

9. Ⓐ bark
   Ⓑ dirt
   Ⓒ straw
   Ⓓ leaves

10. Ⓕ dig a deep hole
    Ⓖ choose a good spot for the tree
    Ⓗ choose a young tree
    Ⓙ add mulch to the soil

STOP

Name ______________________________ Date ______________

# Test 

**Sample A**

Ⓐ illustrate
Ⓑ identify
Ⓒ repeat
Ⓓ put together

**For questions 1–13, darken the circle for the word or words that best complete the sentence you hear.**

**1.** Ⓐ exact
Ⓑ jumbled
Ⓒ wrong
Ⓓ exaggerated

**2.** Ⓕ serious
Ⓖ silly
Ⓗ steady
Ⓙ weary

**3.** Ⓐ mangle
Ⓑ spy
Ⓒ play with
Ⓓ observe

**4.** Ⓕ decrease
Ⓖ stop
Ⓗ increase
Ⓙ advertise

**5.** Ⓐ make
Ⓑ like
Ⓒ suppose
Ⓓ consider

**6.** Ⓕ organize
Ⓖ classify
Ⓗ laugh about
Ⓙ remember

**7.** Ⓐ color
Ⓑ mark
Ⓒ smile
Ⓓ wound

**8.** Ⓕ unbiased
Ⓖ close-minded
Ⓗ colorful
Ⓙ biased

**9.** Ⓐ charming
Ⓑ annoying
Ⓒ delightful
Ⓓ tolerable

**10.** Ⓕ climate
Ⓖ anger
Ⓗ background
Ⓙ nature

**11.** Ⓐ leave
Ⓑ fix
Ⓒ enter
Ⓓ occupy

**12.** Ⓕ hopeless
Ⓖ unconvinced
Ⓗ hopeful
Ⓙ pessimistic

**13.** Ⓐ changeable
Ⓑ constant
Ⓒ expensive
Ⓓ unchangeable

STOP

Name ______________________ Date ______________

**Sample B**

Ⓐ a single line of silk

Ⓑ a cocoon

Ⓒ spider eggs

Ⓓ prey

**For questions 14–24, listen to the passage. Then darken the circle for the word or words that best answer the question.**

**14.** Ⓕ all came from Salisbury, England
Ⓖ are all intact
Ⓗ might have been transported from Wales
Ⓙ were small and smooth

**15.** Ⓐ Scientists can only guess what the monument once looked like.
Ⓑ The monument has been unchanged over the years.
Ⓒ Scientists know exactly how the monument was used.
Ⓓ Scientists know why it was built.

**16.** Ⓕ a building
Ⓖ an ancient monument
Ⓗ an ancient city
Ⓙ a quarry

**17.** Ⓐ Wales
Ⓑ Ireland
Ⓒ Asia
Ⓓ England

**18.** Ⓕ talks about one homeless family
Ⓖ asks for money
Ⓗ offers money for donated items
Ⓙ asks a question

**19.** Ⓐ a house with some furniture
Ⓑ a house with everything a family will need for a year
Ⓒ an empty house
Ⓓ a house that will need many improvements

**20.** Ⓕ call the city to pick up the items
Ⓖ give the items to friends and neighbors
Ⓗ bring the items to the school gym
Ⓙ give the items directly to a homeless family

**21.** Ⓐ rotting roots
Ⓑ the sea
Ⓒ a little house
Ⓓ sunflowers

**22.** Ⓕ bear fur
Ⓖ asters
Ⓗ colorless
Ⓙ extinct

**23.** Ⓐ The wind blows on a prairie.
Ⓑ There are many tall trees on a prairie.
Ⓒ The plants and flowers on a prairie are fed by rotting roots.
Ⓓ Prairie soil is dark and fertile.

**24.** Ⓕ The little house was built on the prairie.
Ⓖ Goldenrod blooms on the prairie.
Ⓗ A prairie blown by the wind looks like a sea of grass.
Ⓙ Pioneers crossed the prairies.

STOP

Name ______________________ Date ______________

# Unit 8: Language

## PREWRITING, COMPOSING, AND EDITING

**Directions: Read each sentence carefully. Then darken the circle for the correct answer to each sentence.**

| **Try This** | Imagine you are writing each sentence. Use the rules you have learned for capitalization, punctuation, word usage, and sentence structure to choose the correct answer. |
|---|---|

**The Costs of Using Tobacco**

Celeste is the editor-in-chief of her school newspaper. She knows of several students in her school who smoke or have started smoking. She decides it is important to write an editorial about the hazards of using tobacco.

**Sample A**

What should Celeste do before she starts to write her editorial?

Ⓐ Find information about tobacco use.

Ⓑ Check the spellings of unfamiliar words.

Ⓒ Make a map showing where tobacco is grown.

Ⓓ Check a thesaurus to find the best words to use.

| **Think It Through** | The correct answer is A. The first thing Celeste should do is find information about her topic. It is important to have a body of factual information to use in order to write a good editorial. |
|---|---|

**While Celeste was writing her editorial, she used the dictionary to check some words.**

nic·o·tine

*n.* A poisonous substance and highly addictive drug that is found in tobacco products.

1. How many syllables does nicotine have?

Ⓐ 2

Ⓑ 3

Ⓒ 4

Ⓓ 5

GO ON

Name ______________________ Date ______________

**Here is a rough draft of the first part of Celeste's editorial. Read the rough draft carefully. Then answer questions 2–9.**

## The Costs of Using Tobacco

In physical education class, yesterday, Justin collapsed the mile **(1)** while running. Justin used to be one of the best runners on our school's **(2)** track team. What had happened? **(3)** Was he sick? **(4)** Had he sprained his **(5)** ankle? Did he skip eating breakfast? **(6)** I had a bowl of oatmeal for **(7)** breakfast. Everyone wondered what had happened to Justin. **(8)** I decided **(9)** to ask him and his answer may surprise you it surprised me.

"I out of breath. **(10)** My lungs were in extreme pain. **(11)** I was coughing, and **(12)** I lost my energy to run." Justin then admitted that he has been smoking **(13)** cigarettes for the past three months. "I'm only smoking half a pack a **(14)** day. I find it hard to believe that smoking that small amount could **(15)** cause me to feel so bad."

2. What is the topic sentence of the first paragraph?
   - Ⓕ 1
   - Ⓖ 2
   - Ⓗ 6
   - Ⓙ 7

3. Which sentence is a run-on sentence?
   - Ⓐ 2
   - Ⓑ 6
   - Ⓒ 7
   - Ⓓ 9

GO ON

**4.** How could sentence 1 be correctly rewritten?

______________________________

______________________________

______________________________

______________________________

______________________________

______________________________

**5.** Which group of words in Celeste's editorial is not a complete sentence?

Ⓕ 3

Ⓖ 6

Ⓗ 10

Ⓙ 12

**6.** What is the most colorful way to write sentence 8?

Ⓐ Everyone wondered why Justin had collapsed.

Ⓑ Everyone wondered what happened to Justin to cause his dramatic collapse in class yesterday.

Ⓒ Everyone wondered what could have happened to Justin in class to make him collapse.

Ⓓ As it is written.

**7.** Combine sentence 10 and sentence 11 into one sentence without changing their meaning.

______________________________

______________________________

______________________________

______________________________

______________________________

______________________________

**8.** Which of the following sentences could be added after sentence 12?

Ⓕ Then I just fell to the ground.

Ⓖ She ran up and tried to stop his fall.

Ⓗ Celeste writes down everything he says.

Ⓙ He tripped on his shoelaces.

**9.** What sentence contains information that does not belong in Celeste's article?

Ⓐ 5

Ⓑ 6

Ⓒ 7

Ⓓ 12

GO ON

Name ______________________ Date ______________

**Here is the next part of Celeste's rough draft for her editorial. This part has certain words and phrases underlined. Read the draft carefully. Then answer questions 10–17.**

(16) I researched <u>the effects of smoking to find out</u>. (17) Did <u>you knew</u> that the nicotine contained in cigarettes can cause beginning smokers to become dizzy? (18) Nicotine is a powerful drug. (19) <u>Nicotine made the heart</u> work harder and beat faster.

(20) <u>When they burn, cigarettes release</u> a gas called carbon monoxide. (21) This gas causes blood vessels to narrow. (22) It also makes it difficult for your blood cells to carry oxygen to body cells and to carry carbon dioxide away from the cells to the lungs. (23) Carbon monoxide is the same gas that comes out of the exhaust pipes of cars. (24) If you inhale too much of this gas, <u>it can kill him</u>.

(25) Another fact that I discovered is that smoking tobacco causes the lungs to work less efficiently. (26) Tar, <u>which is a dense</u>, gummy, dark liquid, attaches to parts of the <u>respiratory tract, and makes it</u> difficult to breathe properly.

(27) I believe the cost of cigarettes is about $2.00 a pack. (28) That sounds like an expensive habit to me. (29) More costly than this, however, is what smoking can cost a person in lost dreams. (30) Justin, is smoking really worth <u>losing its ability</u> to run like the wind?

GO ON

Name ______________________________ Date ______________

**10.** In sentence 16, the effects of smoking to find out is best written —

Ⓕ smoking effects to find out smoking

Ⓖ to find out the effects of smoking

Ⓗ the smoking effects to find out

Ⓙ As it is written.

**11.** In sentence 17, you knew that is best written —

Ⓐ they knew that

Ⓑ you had known

Ⓒ you know that

Ⓓ As it is written.

**12.** In sentence 19, Nicotine made the heart is best written —

Ⓕ Nicotine makes the heart

Ⓖ Nicotine make the heart

Ⓗ Nicotine have made the heart

Ⓙ As it is written.

**13.** In sentence 20, When they burn, cigarettes release is best written —

Ⓐ When they burned, cigarettes, release

Ⓑ When they are burning cigarettes release

Ⓒ Cigarettes, when burned release,

Ⓓ As it is written.

**14.** In sentence 24, it can kill him is best written —

Ⓕ it can kill her

Ⓖ it can kill you

Ⓗ it can kill them

Ⓙ As it is written.

**15.** In sentence 26, respiratory tract, and makes it is best written —

Ⓐ respiratory, tract, and makes it

Ⓑ respiratory tract and, makes it

Ⓒ respiratory tract and makes it

Ⓓ As it is written.

**16.** In sentence 26, which is a dense is best written —

Ⓕ which was a dense

Ⓖ which would have been dense

Ⓗ which is densely

Ⓙ As it is written.

**17.** In sentence 30, losing its ability is best written —

Ⓐ losing their ability

Ⓑ losing your ability

Ⓒ losing her ability

Ⓓ As it is written.

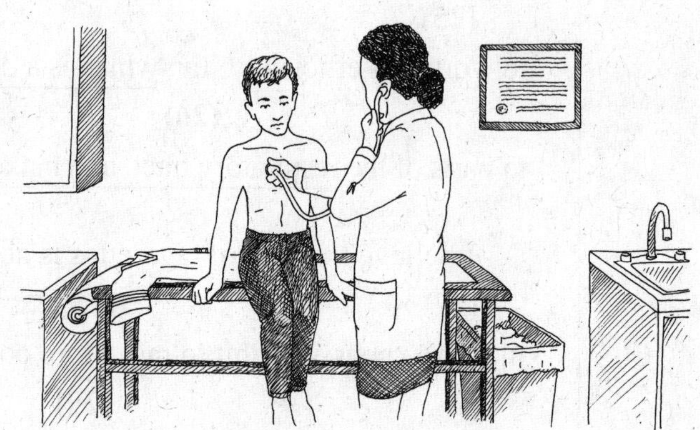

STOP

Name ______________________________ Date ______________

# IDENTIFYING MISSPELLED WORDS

**Directions: Read each sentence carefully. If one of the words is misspelled, darken the circle for that word. If all the words are spelled correctly, then darken the circle for *No mistake.***

| Try This | Read each sentence carefully. If you are not sure of an answer, first decide which answer choices are spelled correctly. Then see if you can recognize the misspelled word from your reading experience. |
|---|---|

**Sample A**

The lens in the microscope magnifyed the object ten times. No mistake
Ⓐ lens Ⓑ magnifyed Ⓒ object Ⓓ No mistake

| Think It Through | The correct answer is B. Magnified is spelled m-a-g-n-i-f-i-e-d. |
|---|---|

1. We were denied acces to the backstage area at the concert. No mistake
Ⓐ denied Ⓑ acces Ⓒ concert Ⓓ No mistake

2. The ornate colums give that house a colonial look. No mistake
Ⓕ ornate Ⓖ colums Ⓗ colonial Ⓙ No mistake

3. She is tenseing up before she swings her racket. No mistake
Ⓐ tenseing Ⓑ swings Ⓒ racket Ⓓ No mistake

4. We heard the wolf's cry eko throughout the canyon. No mistake
Ⓕ eko Ⓖ throughout Ⓗ canyon Ⓙ No mistake

5. The students were bored by the monatonous speech. No mistake
Ⓐ bored Ⓑ monatonous Ⓒ speech Ⓓ No mistake

6. The pilot made an adjustment before landing the plain. No mistake
Ⓕ pilot Ⓖ adjustment Ⓗ plain Ⓙ No mistake

7. Did you notice the message on the bulletin board? No mistake
Ⓐ notice Ⓑ message Ⓒ bulletin Ⓓ No mistake

8. Climbing the mountain from this location is not adviseable. No mistake
Ⓕ Climbing Ⓖ location Ⓗ adviseable Ⓙ No mistake

STOP

Name ______________________________ Date ______________

# TEST

**Sample A**

Mara wants to learn to in-line skate. She cannot find a class that teaches this skill. She decides to write a letter to the office of her park district to suggest that the park district offer in-line skating lessons.

Before she writes the letter, Mara wants to know about the success of in-line skating lessons in other park districts. She should look in —

Ⓐ an atlas.

Ⓑ the *Readers' Guide to Periodical Literature.*

Ⓒ a thesaurus.

Ⓓ an encyclopedia.

**Read the selection below carefully. Then answer questions 1–4.**

## American Impressionists

In art class Pat learned about impressionism, the style of art that shows what a painter sees at a glance. He was intrigued with the way the impressionists used light and its reflection. He was particularly interested in American impressionists and their contributions to this school of painting. Pat decided to use this as the subject of his research paper for English class.

**1.** What should Pat do before he writes his research paper?

Ⓐ check the definitions of words that he might use

Ⓑ make an outline of information to include in the paper

Ⓒ determine the length of the paper

Ⓓ find out what kind of art most people like

**2.** Which topic would <u>not</u> be appropriate for Pat's paper?

Ⓕ famous impressionist painters

Ⓖ a study of light and color

Ⓗ subjects of impressionist paintings

Ⓙ how to arrange paintings at an exhibit

**3.** Where would Pat find general information about impressionism?

Ⓐ the almanac

Ⓑ the dictionary

Ⓒ the encyclopedia

Ⓓ the thesaurus

**4.** Where should Pat look first to find information about American impressionists?

______________________________

______________________________

______________________________

______________________________

GO ON

Name ____________________ Date ____________

**Here is a rough draft of the first part of Pat's research paper. Read the rough draft carefully. Then answer questions 5–10.**

## American Impressionists

(1) Impressionist artists developed their style in the late 1800s. (2) The painter's first impression of the object or event depicted. (3) The impressionists made an effort not to paint what they knew or felt about the subject. (4) They painted just what they saw. (5) The impressionist style of painting simulates light as it looks when it reflects from the surface of things. (6) They used pure color—color that was not mixed on a palette. (7) This gave the paintings a brilliant, vibrant effect.

(8) Although most impressionist painters were from France, artists from many other countries were part of this art movement. (9) The United States was represented by artists such as James A. M. Whistler, Mary Cassatt, John Singer Sargent, and Childe Hassam. (10) All these artists studied impressionist art in Europe.

(11) James A. M. Whistler was born in Lowell, Massachusetts, in 1834. (12) He went to West Point he was forced to leave because of his failing grades in chemistry. (13) Whistler then became a map engraver for the United States Coast Guard. (14) A year later, he quit this job and left for Paris to become an artist. (15) He took the critic to court for slander. (16) There he studied the style of French impressionist painter Henri Fantin-Latour.

GO ON

Name ______________________________ Date ______________

5. Which group of words is not a complete sentence?

Ⓕ 2

Ⓖ 4

Ⓗ 5

Ⓙ 6

6. Combine sentences 3 and 4 into one sentence without changing their meaning.

______________________________

______________________________

______________________________

______________________________

______________________________

______________________________

7. Which of the following sentences could be added after sentence 7?

Ⓐ Americans did not recognize the artistry of impressionist painters.

Ⓑ The impressionist movement lasted for about 50 years.

Ⓒ Impressionism can also be found in sculptures.

Ⓓ The colors in impressionist paintings often have a shimmering quality to them.

8. Which sentence is a run-on sentence?

Ⓕ 6

Ⓖ 9

Ⓗ 12

Ⓙ 13

9. What is the best way to write sentence 11?

Ⓐ In 1834, in Lowell, Massachusetts, was born James A. M. Whistler.

Ⓑ Lowell, Massachusetts, in 1834, James A. M. Whistler was born.

Ⓒ James A. M. Whistler, in Lowell, Massachusetts, in 1834 was born.

Ⓓ As it is written.

10. Which sentence contains information that does not belong in this report?

Ⓕ 9

Ⓖ 10

Ⓗ 14

Ⓙ 15

GO ON

Name ______________________________ Date ______________

**Here is the next part of Pat's rough draft for his research paper. This part has certain words and phrases underlined. Read the draft carefully. Then answer questions 11–18.**

> Mary Cassatt was born in Allegheny, Pennsylvania, in 1844. She was interested from an early age in painting. Cassatt studies art at the Pennsylvania Academy of Fine Arts. She emigrated to France and she became a well-respected member of the French impressionist movement.
>
> **(17)** Mary Cassatt was born in Allegheny, Pennsylvania, in 1844. **(18)** She was interested from an early age in painting. **(19)** Cassatt studies art at the Pennsylvania Academy of Fine Arts. **(20)** She emigrated to France and she became a well-respected member of the French impressionist movement.
>
> **(21)** Cassatt's paintings usually depict people doing routine activities. **(22)** She often chose mothers and children as her subjects. **(23)** Cassatt used light, bright colors and vague brush strokes to create the illusion of what the eye sees at a glance. **(24)** She also occasionally used muted colors and strong, clear lines in their paintings. **(25)** Cassatt encouraged American art collectors to purchase impressionist paintings. **(26)** As a result many impressionist paintings hang in museum galleries in the United States today.
>
> **(27)** I have not never seen any of Cassatt's paintings in person. **(28)** I want to start a club at school called the American impressionist club, whose members could study these paintings together.

**11.** Rewrite sentence 18 correctly.

______________________________

______________________________

______________________________

______________________________

______________________________

**12.** In sentence 19, how could studies art best be rewritten?

______________________________

______________________________

______________________________

______________________________

GO ON

Name ______________________________ Date ______________

**13.** In sentence 20, France and she became is best written —

Ⓐ France and she become

Ⓑ France, and she, became

Ⓒ France and she had become

Ⓓ As it is written.

**14.** In sentence 21, Cassatt's paintings is best written —

Ⓕ Cassatts' paintings

Ⓖ Cassatt paintings'

Ⓗ Cassatts' painting

Ⓙ As it is written.

**15.** In sentence 24, in their paintings is best written —

Ⓐ in her paintings

Ⓑ in they paintings

Ⓒ in paintings of theirs

Ⓓ As it is written.

**16.** In sentence 26, As a result many is best written —

Ⓕ As a result, many

Ⓖ As a result, many,

Ⓗ As a result many,

Ⓙ As it is written.

**17.** In sentence 27, I have not never seen is best written —

Ⓐ I had not never seen

Ⓑ I have never seen

Ⓒ I haven't never seen

Ⓓ As it is written.

**18.** In sentence 28, the American impressionist club is best written —

Ⓕ The American Impressionist club

Ⓖ the american impressionist club

Ⓗ the American Impressionist Club

Ⓙ As it is written.

GO ON

Name ______________________________ Date ______________

**For questions 19–30, read each sentence carefully. If one of the words is misspelled, darken the circle for that word. If all of the words are spelled correctly, then darken the circle for *No mistake.***

**19.** It is uncommen for Gina to turn in an incomplete assignment. No mistake
Ⓐ Ⓑ Ⓒ Ⓓ

**20.** We had a great time at the amusment park yesterday. No mistake
Ⓕ Ⓖ Ⓗ Ⓙ

**21.** The lead karacter in the play wore a cape. No mistake
Ⓐ Ⓑ Ⓒ Ⓓ

**22.** Hiroshi was assessed a fine because of his overdo books. No mistake
Ⓕ Ⓖ Ⓗ Ⓙ

**23.** The chemist analyzed the sample in the laboratory. No mistake
Ⓐ Ⓑ Ⓒ Ⓓ

**24.** The cinnamon bear was hibernateing during the winter months. No mistake
Ⓕ Ⓖ Ⓗ Ⓙ

**25.** I want to acknowledge all of the hard work involved in this project. No mistake
Ⓐ Ⓑ Ⓒ Ⓓ

**26.** Our basketball team plays tonight in the semefinal game. No mistake
Ⓕ Ⓖ Ⓗ Ⓙ

**27.** The professor specifyed that the exam should last for one hour. No mistake
Ⓐ Ⓑ Ⓒ Ⓓ

**28.** Queen Victoria rained over the British Empire for sixty-four years. No mistake
Ⓕ Ⓖ Ⓗ Ⓙ

**29.** That document is written in eraseable ink. No mistake
Ⓐ Ⓑ Ⓒ Ⓓ

**30.** The dangerous old building was condemed by the city. No mistake
Ⓕ Ⓖ Ⓗ Ⓙ

STOP

Name ______________________ Date ______________

# Unit 9: Practice Test 1

## READING COMPREHENSION

You have 35 minutes to complete this test. Use the answer sheet on page 127 to mark your answers.

**Sample A**

Bill looks forward to spring because he plays baseball. During fall and winter, however, he has to sell calendars. The money from the calendar sales pays for his uniform.

What does Bill do before he plays baseball?

Ⓐ practices at the batting cages
Ⓑ sells calendars
Ⓒ shops for a uniform
Ⓓ makes his uniform

**For questions 1–26, carefully read each selection. Then darken the circle for the correct answer.**

### All About Insects

Did you know that there are more than 800,000 species of insects in the world? A few hundred of these are harmful pests. Insects annually destroy more than ten percent of the crops raised in the United States. The worst of these crop pests include Colorado beetles, chinch bugs, and grasshoppers. Colorado beetles damage potatoes, while chinch bugs destroy corn and other crops. Swarms of grasshoppers can completely destroy fields of crops.

Insects can cause other damage. Moths and beetles damage fabrics; flies, ants, and cockroaches spoil food; and termites damage furniture and the structures of buildings.

Harmful pests cause disease and other health problems. Fleas and lice cause pain and tissue damage, and flies can carry germs that cause cholera and typhoid fever. Some insects transmit deadly diseases, such as African sleeping sickness and malaria.

The number of helpful species of insects far outweighs the number of harmful species. Helpful insects include butterflies, moths, bees, flies, and wasps. These insects pollinate fruit trees, vegetables, and flowering plants. Some insects provide products. Honeybees make honey and beeswax. Silk moths produce silk. Other helpful insects feed on destructive insects. Ladybugs eat aphids—insects that damage flowering and food plants.

Perhaps the most important insects are those that serve as a food source. A number of plants, birds, reptiles, and fish eat insects as the main part of their diet. *Entomologists* have discovered about 500 species of insects that people use as a food source. Insects are high in protein, minerals, and vitamins. They are part of the diet of people living in Asia, Africa, and South America. For example, giant water bugs are popular in Asia. In South America, some people buy a species of ant as a treat in movie theaters. In Japan, insect farmers harvest wasps to be cooked, canned, and sold. Today some people in the United States eat fried caterpillars and chocolate-covered bees and ants.

GO ON

Name ________________________________ Date ______________

1. Which insects are considered to be both harmful and helpful?

Ⓐ flies

Ⓑ boll weevils

Ⓒ fleas

Ⓓ lice

2. Which insect is responsible for carrying germs that cause typhoid fever?

Ⓕ Colorado beetles

Ⓖ grasshoppers

Ⓗ fleas

Ⓙ flies

3. According to the selection, how many species of insects are there in the world?

Ⓐ more than 800,000

Ⓑ a few hundred thousand

Ⓒ 500

Ⓓ a few hundred

4. Insects are an important part of the diet of people in Asia, Africa, and South America because insects are high in —

Ⓕ vitamins.

Ⓖ fats.

Ⓗ germs.

Ⓙ calories.

5. This selection was most likely written in order to —

Ⓐ describe the harmful and beneficial effects of insects.

Ⓑ encourage agriculture around the world.

Ⓒ promote the use of silk products.

Ⓓ explain the many ways to prepare insects for meals.

6. The web shows some important ideas in the selection.

Which of these belongs in the empty space?

Ⓕ cause disease

Ⓖ eaten as treats in theaters

Ⓗ produce silk

Ⓙ eat other insects

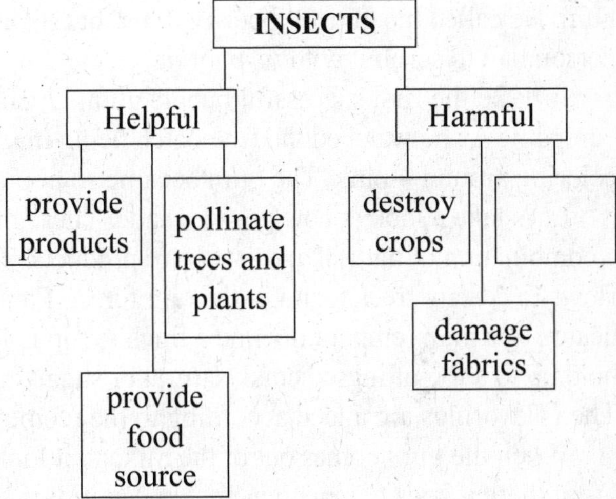


7. What is an *entomologist*?

________________________________________

________________________________________

________________________________________

________________________________________

8. What service do ladybugs provide?

________________________________________

________________________________________

________________________________________

________________________________________

GO ON

Name ____________________ Date ____________

# The History of Chewing Gum

Do you like chewing gum? Millions of people around the world do. It's difficult to imagine a place where people don't chew gum. Chewing gum has been taken up the highest mountain peaks, deep down into the oceans, and even into space.

Chewing gum has been in existence for a long time. It was first enjoyed by the ancient Greeks about a.d. 50. They chewed the sap of the mastic tree. The Mayans of Central America chewed chicle, the resin of the sapodilla tree. When the pilgrims came to North America, Native Americans gave them the resin of spruce trees to chew.

In 1848 John Curtis of Maine manufactured the first gum for sale. The gum sold so well that Curtis built the world's first gum factory and hired 200 workers. In 1906 Frank Fleer came up with the idea of bubble gum. He called his gum Blibber-Blubber, but it was never sold. It was so sticky that if it got on the skin, a person had to scrub it with *turpentine*, or paint thinner, to remove it.

In 1926 the first successful bubble gum, Dubble Bubble, was invented by an accountant at a gum company. As he watched the first batch being made, he realized that it had no color. He grabbed the only coloring around—pink. The gum became so popular that most bubble gum today is still pink.

Let's take a look at how gum is made. There must be a base to make the gum sticky. This base is usually a combination of natural and *synthetic* products. The natural base is made from latex. Latex is the sap that flows in certain trees found in the rain forest. First, the ingredients for the base are mixed together. They are heated to a high temperature and a thick syrup is formed. The syrup is poured into a giant mixer that can hold up to a ton of ingredients. Natural or sugar-free sweeteners are added to make the gum sweet and moist. Then flavorings are added according to the recipe being used.

When the gum comes out of the mixers, it looks like bread dough. It is deposited on belts where it cools. From there it goes to machines that knead it. It is kneaded for a few hours, then cut into rectangular chunks.

If the dough is going to become sheet gum, it is then sent through large rollers that flatten it into thin sheets. The large sheets are cut into small sticks. The sticks are wrapped and sealed. To make bubble gum, the dough is squeezed through a tube. Then it is cut into small balls and wrapped. Finally the gum is ready to be shipped to a store and sold.

Now you know a little about the history of chewing gum and how it is made. But there are many other interesting facts about gum. For example, a dentist in Oregon once helped solve a murder by examining a piece of chewing gum. The suspect said he had never been at the scene of the crime. But his saliva and bite marks on a piece of chewing gum found at the crime scene proved he was not telling the truth.

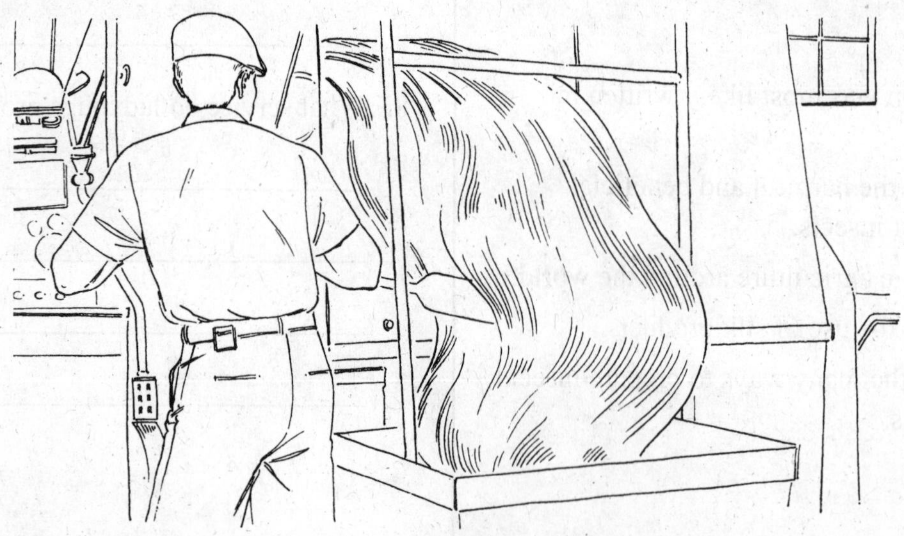

GO ON

Name ______________________________________ Date ____________

9. People who choose to read this selection are probably interested in —

Ⓐ participating in sports.

Ⓑ the history of inventions.

Ⓒ learning accounting methods.

Ⓓ marketing products.

10. The boxes show some directions for making gum.

| The base is made. | Sweeteners are added. | The gum is kneaded. | |
|---|---|---|---|
| 1 | 2 | 3 | 4 |

Which of these belongs in Box 4?

Ⓕ Flavorings are added.

Ⓖ The gum is cut into rectangles.

Ⓗ Syrup is poured into a mixer.

Ⓙ The ingredients are heated to a high temperature.

11. Blibber-Blubber was never sold because —

Ⓐ it was too expensive to buy.

Ⓑ it was too sticky.

Ⓒ it was not the right color.

Ⓓ it was too difficult to make.

12. You can tell the word *turpentine* in this selection means —

Ⓕ paint thinner.

Ⓖ soap.

Ⓗ clothes detergent.

Ⓙ grease.

13. Where was gum first chewed?

Ⓐ in Central America

Ⓑ in North America

Ⓒ in ancient Greece

Ⓓ in Maine

14. A recipe is used for

Ⓕ so that the person n forget to mix the ingre

Ⓖ because the owner of the requires it.

Ⓗ so that the gum will taste the sa time it is made.

Ⓙ so that sticks of gum will always loo the same.

15. You can tell the word *synthetic* means —

Ⓐ necessary.

Ⓑ tinted.

Ⓒ manufactured.

Ⓓ foreign.

16. What is used to make the base of chewing gum?

Ⓕ sweeteners

Ⓖ natural and synthetic products

Ⓗ flavorings

Ⓙ flour

17. Why is most bubble gum pink?

Ⓐ It is illegal to make it any other color.

Ⓑ Other colors do not stick to the gum as well as pink does.

Ⓒ Only pink makes good bubbles.

Ⓓ The first bubble gum was pink and it was very popular.

18. What is the main idea of the last paragraph?

______________________________

______________________________

______________________________

______________________________

GO ON

Date ____________

# Sharon's Birthday Dinner

In Sharon's family, each family member gets to choose his or her favorite birthday meal. Here are the recipes used for Sharon's birthday dinner.

**Stuffed Shrimp Appetizer**

**Ingredients:**

12 cooked shrimp, large to jumbo

$\frac{1}{4}$ cup chives, chopped

1 cup cream cheese

shrimp sauce (to taste)

With a knife, split large-to-jumbo size shrimp open down the back, but not all the way through. Mix chopped chives and cream cheese together. Stuff shrimp with mixture and secure with a toothpick. Pour shrimp sauce, to taste, over shrimp. Refrigerate for one hour before serving.

**Sweet and Sour Salad**

**Ingredients:**

4 cups fresh broccoli or cauliflower, cut into bite-size pieces

8 slices bacon, cooked crisp and crumbled

1 small red onion, chopped

3 tablespoons cider vinegar

1 cup mayonnaise

$\frac{1}{4}$ cup sugar

Pour broccoli into bowl with onion and crumbled bacon. Mix cider vinegar, mayonnaise, and sugar and pour over vegetables. Refrigerate at least a few hours, but overnight is better.

**Swiss Chicken Cutlets**

**Ingredients:**

5 chicken cutlets

1 egg, beaten

1 cup bread crumbs

$\frac{1}{4}$ cup oil

$\frac{1}{4}$ cup flour

$\frac{1}{8}$ teaspoon pepper

3 tablespoons butter or margarine

1 teaspoon salt

$2\frac{1}{3}$ cups milk

1 cup (8 ounces) shredded Swiss cheese

Pound chicken cutlets with mallet. Sprinkle chicken cutlets with salt and dip in beaten egg. Then cover chicken cutlets with bread crumbs. In a frying pan or skillet, brown the breaded chicken cutlets. Set aside.

In a skillet, melt butter and blend in flour, salt, pepper, and milk. Cook mixture until thickened. Remove mixture from heat. Pour half the mixture into a baking pan. Arrange chicken cutlets on top. Then pour the remaining mixture over the chicken cutlets. Sprinkle the Swiss cheese on top. Bake in the oven at 350°F for 50 minutes.

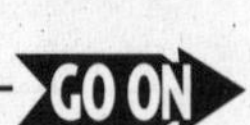

Name ______________________ Date ______________

19. In the recipe for stuffed shrimp, the phrase "not all the way through" means —

Ⓕ partially cook the shrimp.

Ⓖ cut the shrimp part of the way without cutting it into two halves.

Ⓗ refrigerate the shrimp before cooking.

Ⓙ mix together only half the chives and cream cheese.

20. What do you need in order to make the appetizer?

Ⓐ a measuring spoon

Ⓑ a grater

Ⓒ a knife

Ⓓ a baking pan

21. What could be substituted for broccoli in the Sweet and Sour Salad?

Ⓕ bacon

Ⓖ red onion

Ⓗ cauliflower

Ⓙ chives

22. If you didn't have a mallet for the chicken recipe, you could use —

Ⓐ a can opener.

Ⓑ a heavy wooden spoon.

Ⓒ a measuring cup.

Ⓓ a baking pan.

23. Another good name for "Swiss Chicken Cutlets" is —

Ⓕ "Spinach Noodles with Chicken."

Ⓖ "Breaded Chicken and Cheese."

Ⓗ "Chicken and Potato Bake."

Ⓙ "Chicken in Mushroom Gravy."

24. What two ingredients in the salad recipe make the dish "sweet and sour?"

______________________

______________________

______________________

______________________

25. You need all the following to make the Swiss Chicken Cutlets *except* —

Ⓐ an egg beater.

Ⓑ a measuring spoon.

Ⓒ a skillet.

Ⓓ a spatula.

26. What step needs to be done just before baking the chicken?

______________________

______________________

______________________

______________________

STOP

Name ______________________________ Date ______________

# Unit 10: Practice Test 2

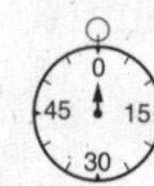


You have 20 minutes to complete this test. Use the answer sheets on page 127 to mark your answers.

## READING VOCABULARY

**Sample A**

Something that is reinforced is —

Ⓐ purchased.
Ⓑ strengthened.
Ⓒ burned.
Ⓓ emptied.

**For questions 1–9, darken the circle for the word or group of words that has the same or almost the same meaning as the underlined word.**

1. An autograph is —
   Ⓐ a photograph.
   Ⓑ an address.
   Ⓒ a telephone number.
   Ⓓ a signature.

2. A haven is a —
   Ⓕ safe place.
   Ⓖ landing field.
   Ⓗ hospital.
   Ⓙ busy highway.

3. A person who is valiant is —
   Ⓐ meek.
   Ⓑ wealthy.
   Ⓒ weak.
   Ⓓ courageous.

4. Something that is revised is —
   Ⓕ altered.
   Ⓖ composed.
   Ⓗ interrupted.
   Ⓙ interpreted.

5. To singe is to —
   Ⓐ chop finely.
   Ⓑ scrub harshly.
   Ⓒ laugh loudly.
   Ⓓ burn slightly.

6. A petition is a kind of —
   Ⓕ charity.
   Ⓖ request.
   Ⓗ poison.
   Ⓙ conference.

7. A grievance is a —
   Ⓐ funeral.
   Ⓑ pain.
   Ⓒ complaint.
   Ⓓ sadness.

8. To administer is to —
   Ⓕ manage.
   Ⓖ play.
   Ⓗ neglect.
   Ⓙ mismanage.

9. Something that is fictitious is —
   Ⓐ heroic.
   Ⓑ imaginary.
   Ⓒ adventurous.
   Ⓓ real.

GO ON

Name ______________________________ Date ______________

**Sample B**

She took a direct flight to Denver.

IIn which sentence does direct have the same meaning as it does in the sentence above?

Ⓐ This is the most direct route home.

Ⓑ Mr. Arnold will direct the choir.

Ⓒ He is a direct descendant of George Washington.

Ⓓ Could you direct me to the library?

**For questions 10–14, darken the circle for the sentence in which the underlined word means the same as it does in the sentence in the box.**

**10.** The school board will discuss that issue tonight.

In which sentence does issue have the same meaning as it does in the sentence above?

Ⓕ Where is the March issue of this magazine?

Ⓖ The city's attorney will issue a statement.

Ⓗ Recycling is a very important issue.

Ⓙ The sergeant will issue clean uniforms in an hour.

**11.** Karl ran the last lap of the relay race.

In which sentence does lap have the same meaning as it does in the sentence above?

Ⓐ The kitten began to lap the milk.

Ⓑ Ryan held the baby gently in his lap.

Ⓒ The horse stumbled during the third lap of the race.

Ⓓ The waves began to lap against the side of the boat.

**12.** Do you know how to prune that tree?

In which sentence does prune have the same meaning as it does in the sentence above?

Ⓕ Amanda refused to eat the prune.

Ⓖ Jenna would have to prune the budget before it would get approved.

Ⓗ Prune away the extra decorations, please.

Ⓙ If you prune the bush, it will have more abundant fruit next year.

**13.** That dress will appeal to her.

In which sentence does appeal have the same meaning as it does in the sentence above?

Ⓐ The mayor will appeal to the citizens of the city to remain calm in the crisis.

Ⓑ The attorney will appeal the case to a higher court.

Ⓒ Does that restaurant appeal to you?

Ⓓ I will appeal to her to go with me.

**14.** You need to draw two parallel lines.

In which sentence does parallel have the same meaning as it does in the sentence above?

Ⓕ Rita's career seems to parallel that of her mother's.

Ⓖ Hiking through the beautiful mountainside has no parallel.

Ⓗ Please park your car between the parallel stripes on the pavement.

Ⓙ The twins have parallel interests.

GO ON

Name ______________________________ Date ______________

**Sample C**

Khalid acted as host and conducted our monthly meeting. Conducted means —

- Ⓐ discovered.
- Ⓑ vacationed.
- Ⓒ directed.
- Ⓓ stored.

STOP

**For questions 15–22, darken the circle for the word or words that give the meaning of the underlined word.**

**15.** The king issued a proclamation stating that everyone in the kingdom had to pay the new tax. Proclamation means —

- Ⓐ report.
- Ⓑ law.
- Ⓒ announcement.
- Ⓓ letter.

**16.** Jill was upset because the same dream was recurring every night. Recurring means —

- Ⓕ repeating.
- Ⓖ shining.
- Ⓗ ringing.
- Ⓙ matching.

**17.** She treated him with disdain. Disdain means —

- Ⓐ respect.
- Ⓑ scorn.
- Ⓒ great care.
- Ⓓ anger.

**18.** The police assured her that it was merely a routine investigation. Routine means —

- Ⓕ short.
- Ⓖ serious.
- Ⓗ regular.
- Ⓙ prison.

**19.** His pompous behavior embarrasses everyone. Pompous means —

- Ⓐ modest.
- Ⓑ arrogant.
- Ⓒ simple.
- Ⓓ polite.

**20.** There was an urgency in her voice that made us worry. Urgency means —

- Ⓕ harsh edge.
- Ⓖ demand for immediate action.
- Ⓗ lack of depth.
- Ⓙ legal decision.

**21.** She had a sedentary job that required little travel. Sedentary means —

- Ⓐ energetic.
- Ⓑ inactive.
- Ⓒ active.
- Ⓓ exciting.

**22.** Because she ran a red light, Rachel was held liable for the car accident. Liable means —

- Ⓕ innocent.
- Ⓖ exempt.
- Ⓗ insensitive.
- Ⓙ responsible.

STOP

Name ______________________________ Date ______________

# Unit 11: Practice Test 3

You have 50 minutes to complete this test. Use the answer sheet on page 128 to mark your answers.

## PART 1: MATH PROBLEM SOLVING

**Sample A**

What is the value of the 6 in 273.0462?

Ⓐ 6 hundredths
Ⓑ 6 thousandths
Ⓒ 6 ten-thousandths
Ⓓ 6 millionths

**For questions 1–47, darken the circle for the correct answer, or write in the answer.**

1. Four people compared the amounts of berries in their buckets. Juan's bucket was $\frac{2}{3}$ full. Jamie's was $\frac{4}{5}$ full, Barb's was $\frac{1}{2}$ full, and Hazel's was $\frac{3}{8}$ full. How would these amounts be arranged from greatest to least?

Ⓐ $\frac{2}{3}, \frac{3}{8}, \frac{4}{5}, \frac{1}{2}$
Ⓑ $\frac{4}{5}, \frac{2}{3}, \frac{1}{2}, \frac{3}{8}$
Ⓒ $\frac{1}{2}, \frac{3}{8}, \frac{4}{5}, \frac{2}{3}$
Ⓓ $\frac{3}{8}, \frac{1}{2}, \frac{2}{3}, \frac{4}{5}$

2. Six hours ago the temperature in Fargo, North Dakota, was $-23°$. Since then, the temperature has risen 20 degrees. What is the current temperature?

______________________________

3. What is the value of point C on the number line?

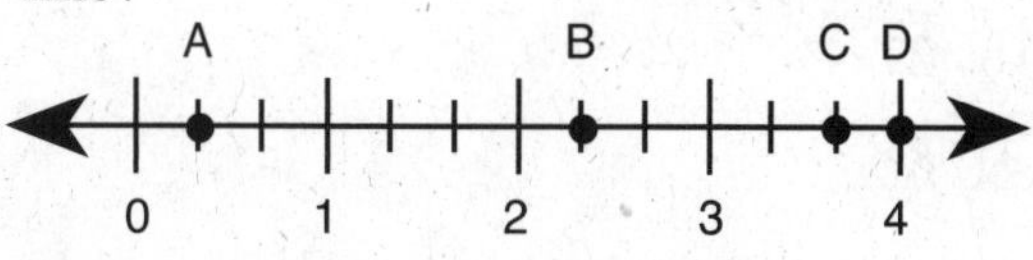


Ⓕ $2\frac{1}{3}$
Ⓗ $3\frac{2}{3}$
Ⓖ $\frac{1}{3}$
Ⓙ 4

4. One estimate for the distance from Earth to the Andromeda Galaxy is 2,300,000 light years. What is this distance expressed in scientific notation?

Ⓐ $2.3 \times 10^5$
Ⓒ $2.3 \times 10^6$
Ⓑ $23 \times 10^5$
Ⓓ $2.3 \times 10^7$

5. If a cave explorer enters a cave at ground level, follows a passage 45 feet underground, then takes a turn and follows another passage up for 23 feet, where would the person be, relative to ground level?

Ⓕ 68 feet
Ⓗ $-22$ feet
Ⓖ 34 feet
Ⓙ $-45$ feet

6. Which fraction is not equivalent to the others in the group?

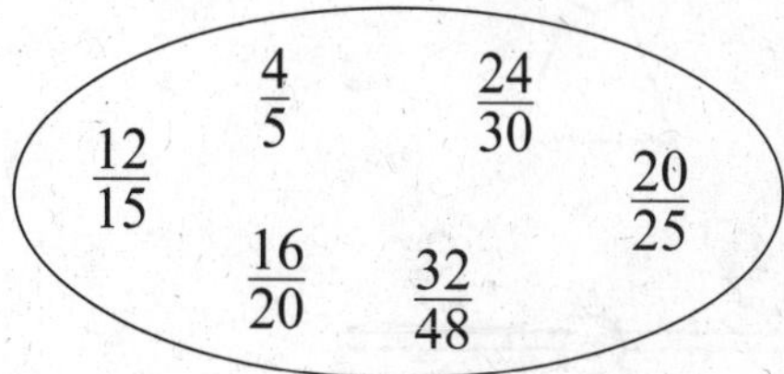


Ⓐ $\frac{24}{30}$
Ⓒ $\frac{20}{25}$
Ⓑ $\frac{12}{15}$
Ⓓ $\frac{32}{48}$

7. Matt mowed $\frac{5}{8}$ of the lawn and then stopped to eat lunch. What percent of the lawn has been mowed?

Ⓕ 58.5%
Ⓗ 67.5%
Ⓖ 62.5%
Ⓙ 87.5%

GO ON

Name ______________________________ Date ______________

8. Four friends wanted to share a pizza. The basic price for a plain cheese pizza is \$8.75. Each additional topping costs \$0.75. The friends ordered a pizza with pepperoni, mushrooms, and onions. Which expression shows what each person paid?

Ⓐ $\frac{8.75}{4} + \frac{75}{3}$

Ⓑ $8.75 \div 4 + \frac{(3 \times 0.75)}{4}$

Ⓒ $\frac{(8.75 + 0.75)}{4}$

Ⓓ $(3 \times 4) + (8.75 + 0.75)$

9. Which of the scales shown here is correctly balanced?

Ⓕ 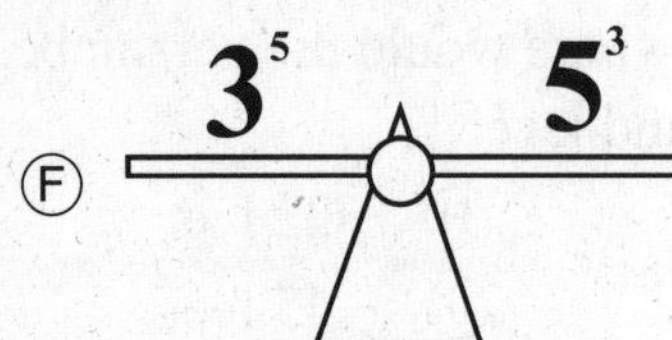


Ⓖ 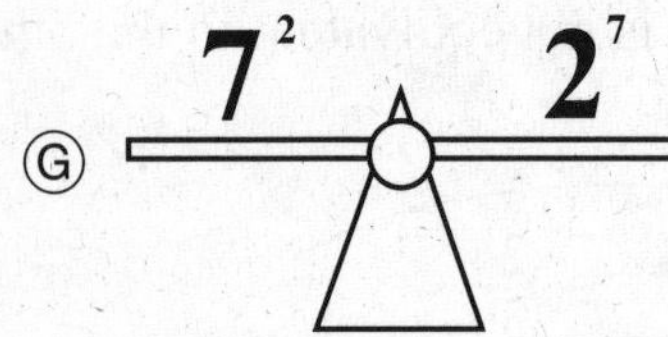


Ⓗ 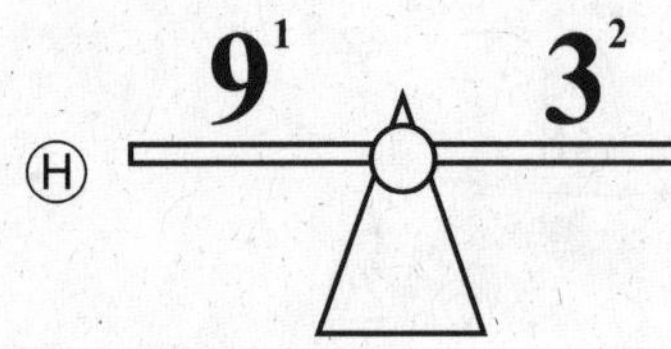


Ⓙ 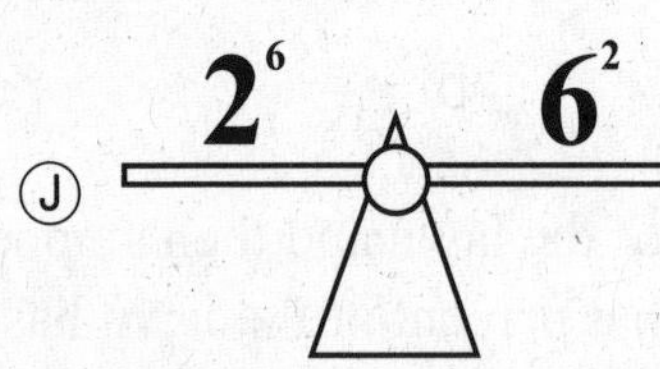


10. Which symbol makes this statement true?
7 yards ___ 7 meters

Ⓐ >

Ⓑ <

Ⓒ =

Ⓓ ≥

11. Which decimal represents the shaded part of the figure?

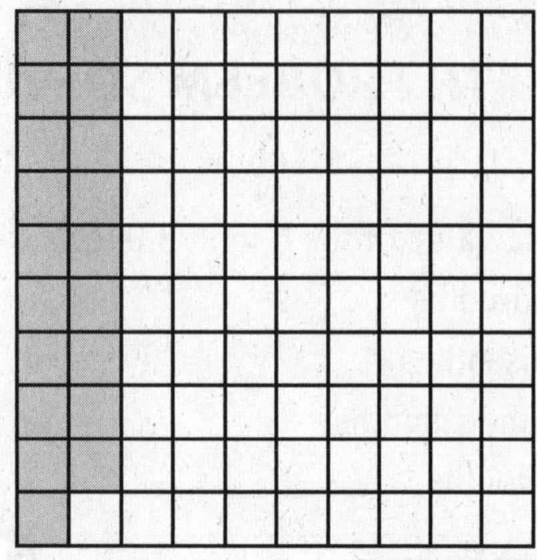

Ⓕ 1.9 Ⓗ 0.019

Ⓖ 0.19 Ⓙ 0.0019

12. The sum of two numbers is 68. One of the numbers is 14 less than the other number. Which of the following equations could be used to find the two numbers?

Ⓐ $\frac{68}{n} = n + 14$

Ⓑ $68 = n + (n - 14)$

Ⓒ $68 \div 14 = n + n$

Ⓓ $68n = n + 14$

13. Which block is in the wrong group?

**Primes** **Composites**

Ⓕ 61

Ⓖ 44

Ⓗ 27

Ⓙ 8

GO ON

Name ______________________________ Date ______________

**14.** Last weekend, Gary and Carol collected aluminum cans for recycling. The expression $g = \frac{c}{2}$ shows the relationship between the number of cans Gary ($g$) collected and the number of cans Carol ($c$) collected. If Gary collected 438 cans, how many did Carol collect?

Ⓐ 219

Ⓑ 336

Ⓒ 657

Ⓓ 876

**15.** A group of hikers planned to take 4 days to climb to the top of a mountain that is 9,753 feet high. The first night they camped $\frac{2}{3}$ of the way up the mountain. Which expression could be used to find *D*, the distance they had left to reach the top of the mountain?

Ⓕ $D = (9{,}753 \div 4) \times 2$

Ⓖ $D = (1 - \frac{2}{3}) + 9{,}753$

Ⓗ $D = 9{,}753 \div (4 - \frac{2}{3})$

Ⓙ $D = 9{,}753 - (\frac{2}{3} \times 9{,}753)$

**16.** Fill in the numbers in Row 6.

| | | | | | | |
|---|---|---|---|---|---|---|
| | | | | | 1 | Row 1 |
| | | | | 3 | 5 | Row 2 |
| | | | 7 | 9 | 11 | Row 3 |
| | | 13 | 15 | 17 | 19 | Row 4 |
| | 21 | 23 | 25 | 27 | 29 | Row 5 |
| | | | | | | Row 6 |

**17.** In the table below, find the missing value of $x$ for the given function.

| $x$ | $\frac{x}{6} + 2$ |
|---|---|
| 3 | $2\frac{1}{2}$ |
| 12 | |
| 0 | 2 |
| | 14 |
| −6 | 1 |

Ⓐ 2, 36

Ⓑ 4, 72

Ⓒ 6, 24

Ⓓ 6, 48

**18.** The graph shows the results of the recent city council elections. If 330,000 people voted, how many people voted for Martinez?

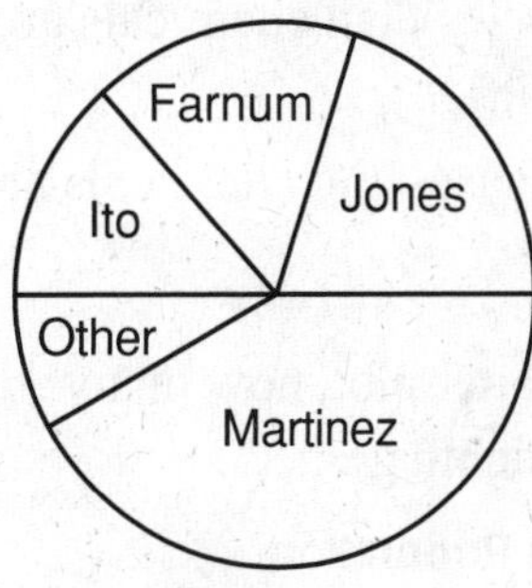


Ⓕ 75,000

Ⓖ 105,000

Ⓗ 180,000

Ⓙ 250,000

**19.** In a recent marshmallow-eating contest, the winner ate 30 marshmallows in 5 minutes. At that rate, how many marshmallows would the winner eat if the contest lasted 20 minutes?

______________________________

______________________________

GO ON

Name ______________________________ Date ______________

**20.** What can be concluded from the information in the graph?

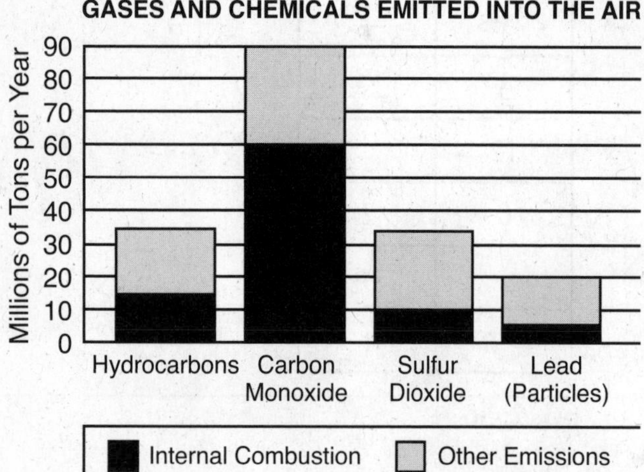


Ⓐ Gases enter the air through three main sources.

Ⓑ Internal combustion engines release millions of tons of gases and chemicals into the air.

Ⓒ More lead particles than chemicals are present in the air.

Ⓓ Relatively few gases and chemicals are present in the air.

**21.** According to the scatter plot, how many students are in the eighth grade?

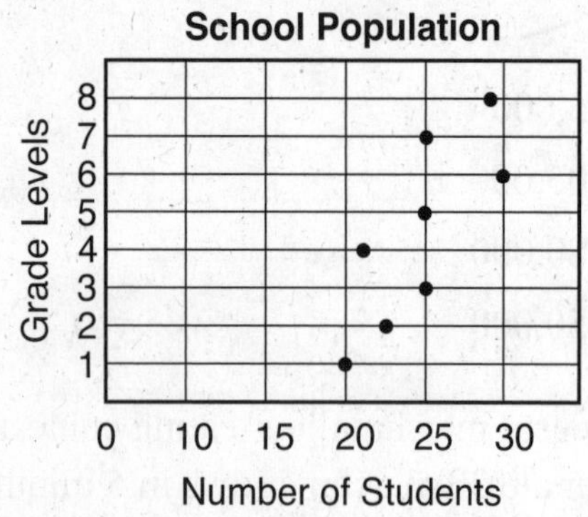


______________________________

______________________________

**22.** If digits cannot be repeated, how many 3-digit numbers can be formed using only the digits 3, 5, 6, 8, and 9?

Ⓕ 5 Ⓗ 36

Ⓖ 24 Ⓙ 60

**23.** What is the average (mean) amount of time spent reading each week by this group?

| Weekly Reading Chart | |
|---|---|
| **Hours** | **Number of Students** |
| 1 | 6 |
| 2 | 12 |
| 3 | 18 |
| 4 | 4 |

______________________________

______________________________

**24.** A bag contains 10 colored cubes. Without looking into the bag, Richard drew out a cube and then replaced it in the bag. He did this 10 times and recorded the results in the table shown here. What conclusion can be drawn from this information?

| Blue | Red | Yellow |
|---|---|---|
| 7 | 1 | 2 |

Ⓐ There is an equal number of blue, red, and yellow cubes in the bag.

Ⓑ There are probably more blue cubes than other colors of cubes.

Ⓒ There are only three colors of cubes in the bag.

Ⓓ There are more than three colors of cubes in the bag.

GO ON

Name ______________________________ Date ______________

**John Eagle Feather took a survey of his class and made a frequency table showing the number of hours his classmates spent on homework each night. Use the table to answer questions 25 though 27.**

| Number of Hours Spent on Homework |
|---|
| 2 2 3 1 1 1 0 3 2 0 4 2 1 3 1 1 2 2 2 3 |

**25.** According to the table, how many students were included in the survey?

______________________________

______________________________

**26.** Which tally chart correctly shows the data in the table above?

Ⓕ
<table>
<tr><td>0</td><td>||</td></tr>
<tr><td>1</td><td>𝍸</td></tr>
<tr><td>2</td><td>|||</td></tr>
<tr><td>3</td><td>|||</td></tr>
<tr><td>4</td><td>|</td></tr>
</table>

Ⓗ
<table>
<tr><td>0</td><td>|||</td></tr>
<tr><td>1</td><td>||||</td></tr>
<tr><td>2</td><td>𝍸</td></tr>
<tr><td>3</td><td>|||</td></tr>
<tr><td>4</td><td>|||</td></tr>
</table>

Ⓖ
<table>
<tr><td>0</td><td>|||</td></tr>
<tr><td>1</td><td>||||</td></tr>
<tr><td>2</td><td>||</td></tr>
<tr><td>3</td><td>𝍸</td></tr>
<tr><td>4</td><td>||</td></tr>
</table>

Ⓙ
<table>
<tr><td>0</td><td>||</td></tr>
<tr><td>1</td><td>𝍸 |</td></tr>
<tr><td>2</td><td>𝍸 ||</td></tr>
<tr><td>3</td><td>||||</td></tr>
<tr><td>4</td><td>|</td></tr>
</table>

**27.** What is the probability that a student spent 1 hour on homework?

Ⓐ $\frac{2}{5}$  Ⓒ $\frac{3}{20}$

Ⓑ $\frac{3}{5}$  Ⓓ $\frac{3}{10}$

**28.** Which figure below has the same number of faces as the figure shown here?

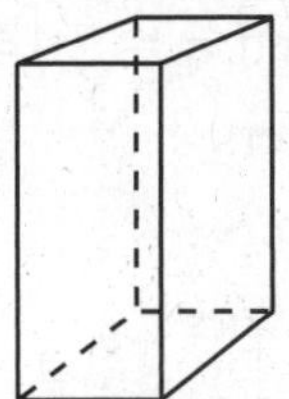

Ⓕ 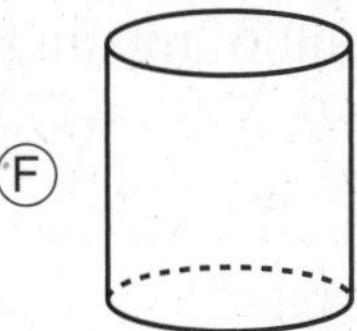

Ⓖ 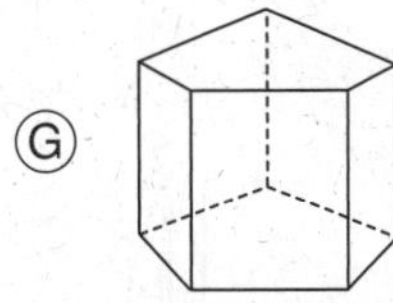

Ⓗ 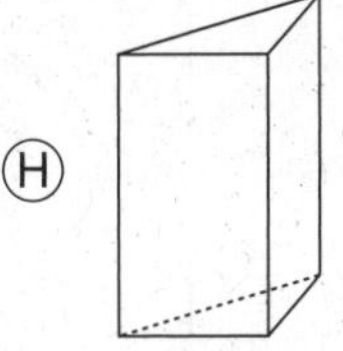

Ⓙ 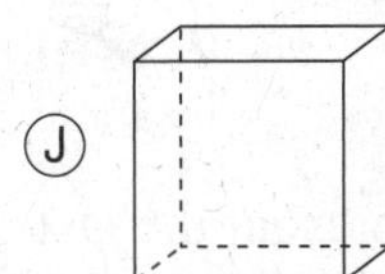

**29.** How much gravel would be needed to fill 75% of the container shown here?

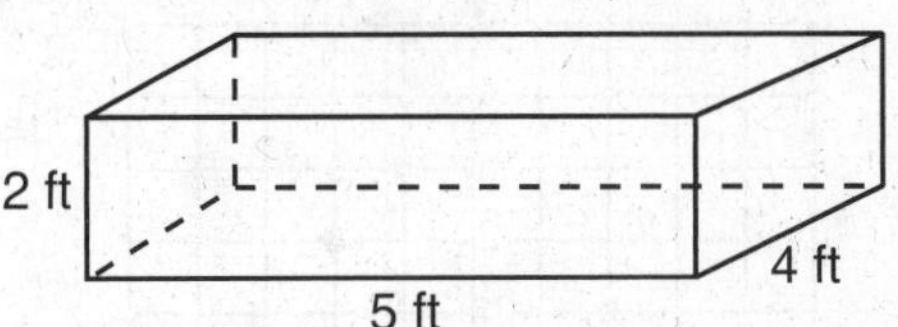


Ⓐ 36 cubic feet

Ⓑ 30 cubic feet

Ⓒ 24 cubic feet

Ⓓ 16 cubic feet

GO ON

Name ______________________________ Date ______________

**30** The face of a wrist watch has a diameter of 28 millimeters. What is its approximate circumference?
(Use $C = 2\pi r$ and $\pi = 3.14$.)

Ⓕ 44 millimeters
Ⓖ 88 millimeters
Ⓗ 615 millimeters
Ⓙ 2,461 millimeters

**31** Which figure shows the result of rotating the tennis shoe 180°?

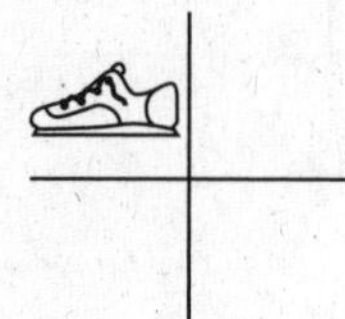

Ⓐ 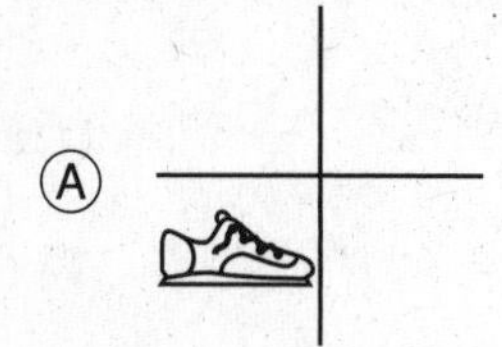

Ⓒ 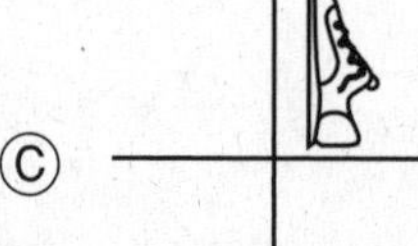

Ⓑ 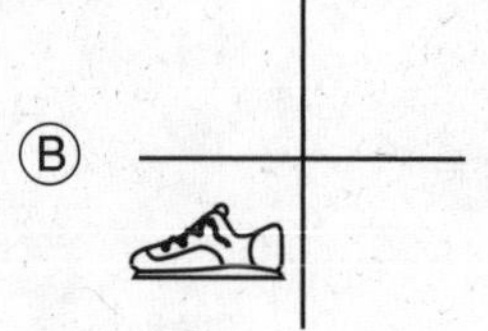

Ⓓ 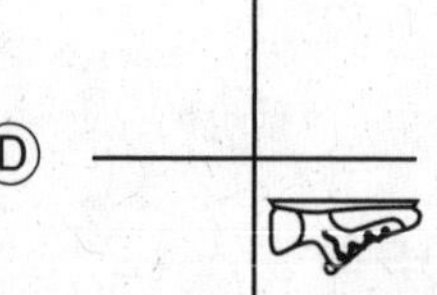

**32** Which coordinates best represent the last point needed to complete the vertices of a rectangle?

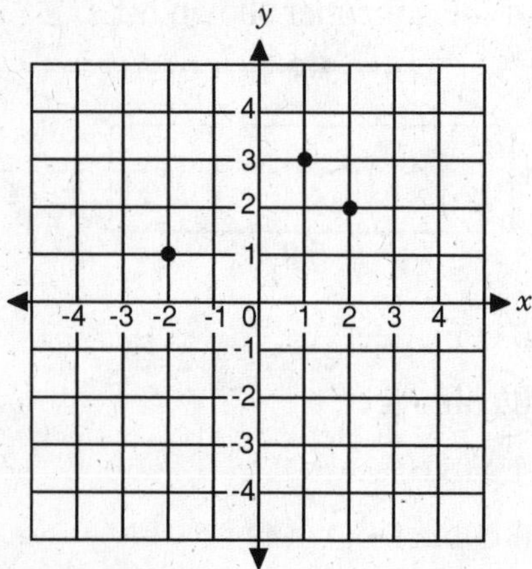


Ⓕ (-1, 0)
Ⓖ ( 0, 0)
Ⓗ (-3, 3)
Ⓙ (1, -1)

**33** The figure shows the circular path covered by a lawn sprinkler. What is the approximate area covered by the sprinkler? (Use $A = \pi r^2$ and $\pi = 3.14$.)

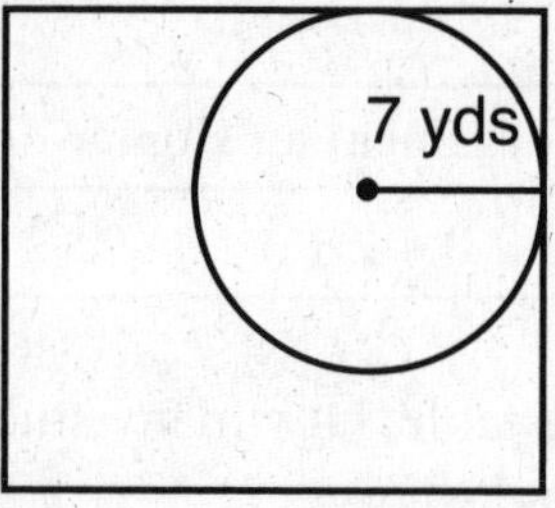


Ⓐ 154 square yards
Ⓑ 128 square yards
Ⓒ 65 square yards
Ⓓ 49 square yards

**34** In the figure shown here, P is the center of the circle. Line segment *AP* is 3 centimeters and line segment *AB* is 4 centimeters. What is the diameter of the circle?

Ⓕ 1.5 centimeters
Ⓖ 3 centimeters
Ⓗ 6 centimeters
Ⓙ 7 centimeters

**35** Which of these numbers has no line segments that are parallel?

**11 14**
**12 77**

______________________________

______________________________

GO ON

Name ________________________________ Date ________________

**Television station WSTB in Clear Valley broadcasts within a 150-mile range.**

**Use your inch ruler to help answer question 36.**

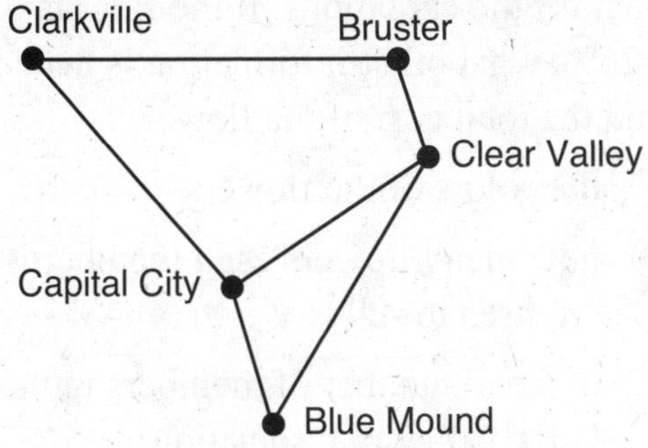


**1 inch = 50 miles**

**36.** Which town or towns can receive WSTB's television broadcasts?

Ⓐ Blue Mound only

Ⓑ Bruster and Blue Mound only

Ⓒ Capital City, Bruster, and Blue Mound only

Ⓓ Clarkville, Capital City, Bruster, and Blue Mound

**37.** Use your centimeter ruler to answer this question. What is the area of this triangle? (Use $A = \frac{1}{2}bh$.)

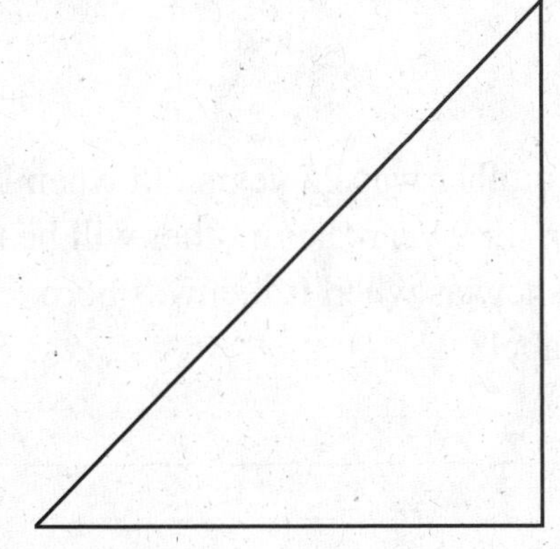

Ⓕ $25\text{ cm}^2$　　Ⓗ $6.25\text{ cm}^2$

Ⓖ $12.5\text{ cm}^2$　　Ⓙ $5.5\text{ cm}^2$

**38.** The McGill's electric bill varies between \$77 and \$84 a month. What would be the best estimate of their electric bill for the next 11 months?

Ⓐ \$80

Ⓑ \$100

Ⓒ \$800

Ⓓ \$1,000

**39.** Patty hiked 5,600 meters around the lake. How many kilometers did Patty hike?

Ⓕ 0.560

Ⓖ 5.6

Ⓗ 56

Ⓙ 560

**40.** Which is closest to the measure of the angle formed by Main Street and First Street?

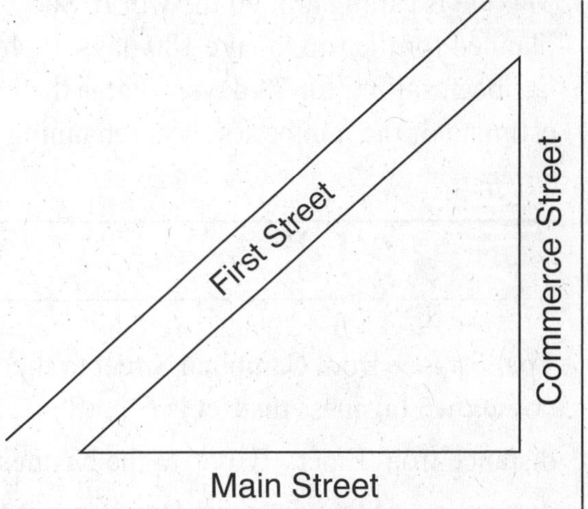


Ⓐ 10°

Ⓑ 45°

Ⓒ 90°

Ⓓ 130°

GO ON

Name ____________________ Date ____________________

**41.** A model car is built on a scale of 1 centimeter = 0.25 meters. If the actual car is 4.5 meters long, how long is the model?

Ⓕ 18 centimeters

Ⓖ 29.5 centimeters

Ⓗ 45 centimeters

Ⓙ 45.5 centimeters

**42.** Of the 40 members of the school track team, 45% are in the seventh and eighth grades, 35% are in the sixth grade, and 20% are in the fifth grade. How many members are in the sixth grade?

Ⓐ 8

Ⓑ 14

Ⓒ 18

Ⓓ 26

**43.** Maxine is sailing around the world. She planned for the trip to take 180 days. If she has been sailing for 78 days, what is the best estimate of the number of days remaining?

____________________

____________________

**44.** The distance from Campbell Street to the downtown business district is $6\frac{3}{4}$ miles. The distance from Emery Drive to the business district is $\frac{1}{4}$ of that distance. How far is it from Emery Drive to the business district?

Ⓕ $1\frac{11}{16}$ miles

Ⓖ $6\frac{1}{2}$ miles

Ⓗ 7 miles

Ⓙ 27 miles

**45.** To raise funds for a special project, the Girls' Athletic Association ordered 450 flowers from a nursery to sell at school. The nursery charged $0.35 each for the daisies and $0.45 each for the carnations. If the sales tax is 7.25%, what other information is needed to find the total cost of the flowers?

Ⓐ the colors of the flowers

Ⓑ how many flowers each member is required to sell

Ⓒ the total number of members in the Girls' Athletic Association

Ⓓ how many of each kind of flower was ordered

**46.** The science class collected 5 tomatoes from the plants they grew in the school greenhouse. The weights are listed in the table below. What is the missing weight?

**Samples**

| A | B | C | D | E | Mean |
|---|---|---|---|---|---|
| 266 | 127 | 562 | | 490 | 359 |

**Weight measured in grams**

Ⓕ 139

Ⓖ 232

Ⓗ 350

Ⓙ 435

**47.** Isabel's mother was 25 years old when Isabel was born. In 9 years her mother will be twice the age she was when Isabel was born. How old is Isabel?

____________________

____________________

STOP

Name ________________________________ Date ____________

## PART 2: MATH PROCEDURES

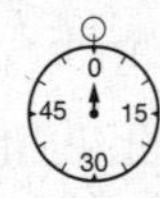

You have 15 minutes to complete this test. Use the answer sheet on page 128 to mark your answers.

**Sample A**

$213 \times .03 =$

Ⓐ 0.639
Ⓑ 6.39
Ⓒ 63.09
Ⓓ 639
Ⓔ NH

STOP

**Sample B**

Julio can save \$12.50 a week from his allowance and paper route. How much money will he have saved after 6 weeks?

Ⓕ \$2.25
Ⓖ \$16.75
Ⓗ \$28
Ⓙ \$75
Ⓚ NH

STOP

**For questions 1–14, darken the circle for the correct answer. Darken the circle for *NH, Not Here,* if the correct answer is not given. If no choices are given, write in your answer.**

**1.** $\frac{7}{9} - \frac{1}{3} =$

Ⓐ $\frac{4}{9}$
Ⓑ 1
Ⓒ $\frac{2}{3}$
Ⓓ $1\frac{1}{3}$
Ⓔ NH

**2.** $9 + (-15) + 3 =$

Ⓕ $-3$
Ⓖ 3
Ⓗ $-6$
Ⓙ 27
Ⓚ NH

**3.** $0.15 \div 0.8 =$

Ⓐ 0.7
Ⓑ 0.23
Ⓒ 0.1875
Ⓓ 1.875
Ⓔ NH

**4.** $\frac{5}{8} \div 8 =$

Ⓕ $8\frac{2}{3}$
Ⓖ $6\frac{2}{3}$
Ⓗ $\frac{5}{48}$
Ⓙ $\frac{5}{14}$
Ⓚ NH

**5.** $11 \times (-9) =$

Ⓐ 99
Ⓑ $-2$
Ⓒ $-20$
Ⓓ $-99$
Ⓔ NH

**6.** $4\frac{2}{3} \times \frac{1}{8} =$

Ⓕ $4\frac{7}{8}$
Ⓖ $4\frac{1}{12}$
Ⓗ $\frac{15}{11}$
Ⓙ $\frac{2}{3}$
Ⓚ NH

**7.** $16 \div \frac{4}{5} =$

Ⓐ $16\frac{1}{5}$
Ⓑ $16\frac{4}{5}$
Ⓒ $12\frac{4}{5}$
Ⓓ 20
Ⓔ NH

**8.**

$$\begin{array}{r} 5\frac{1}{8} \\ +\ 3\frac{3}{4} \\ \hline \end{array}$$

Ⓕ $8\frac{1}{24}$
Ⓖ $9\frac{1}{3}$
Ⓗ $8\frac{7}{8}$
Ⓙ $8\frac{1}{3}$
Ⓚ NH

GO ON

Name ______________________ Date ______________

**9.** Jane spent 6 hours preparing her research paper. She wrote for $3\frac{1}{2}$ hours and then edited her work for 1 hour. She spent the remaining time typing. How many hours did Jane spend typing?

Ⓐ $1\frac{1}{2}$ hours

Ⓑ 2 hours

Ⓒ $2\frac{1}{2}$ hours

Ⓓ 3 hours

Ⓔ NH

**10.** Myra saved 20% off the price of a pair of shoes that cost $46. How much money did Myra save?

Ⓕ $2.75

Ⓖ $5.25

Ⓗ $7.85

Ⓙ $9.20

Ⓚ NH

**11.** Lenore saved $2,500 for a down payment on a car. If the down payment turned out to be only $2,165, how much money did she have left?

______________________

______________________

______________________

______________________

**12.** Sheila spent $8.50 on gas to travel 160 miles. How much would she spend to travel 1,200 miles?

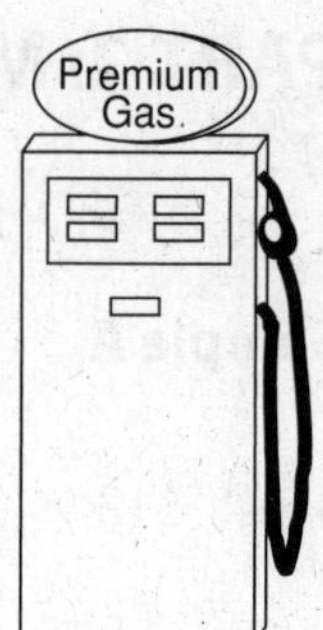


______________________

______________________

______________________

**13.** Paula baby-sat 3 hours on Saturday and 4 hours on Sunday. She earns $4 per hour. How much money did Paula earn in all?

Ⓐ $11

Ⓑ $28

Ⓒ $18

Ⓓ $16

Ⓔ NH

**14.** At the end of the track season, there was only 56% of the original team members left on the girls' varsity track team. What is 56% rounded to the nearest fraction?

Ⓕ $\frac{2}{5}$

Ⓖ $\frac{3}{5}$

Ⓗ $\frac{3}{25}$

Ⓙ $\frac{1}{2}$

Ⓚ NH

STOP

Name ______________________ Date ______________

# Unit 12: Practice Test 4 

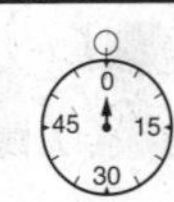

You have 25 minutes to complete this test. Use the answer sheets in the back of the book to mark your answers.

## LISTENING

**Sample A**
Ⓐ foreign
Ⓑ quiet
Ⓒ helpful
Ⓓ unfriendly

**For questions 1–17, darken the circle for the word(s) that best complete the sentence you hear.**

1. Ⓐ worries
Ⓑ travels
Ⓒ swims
Ⓓ writes

2. Ⓕ cheerful
Ⓖ conceited
Ⓗ talented
Ⓙ lonely

3. Ⓐ rope
Ⓑ bottle
Ⓒ barrel
Ⓓ bag

4. Ⓕ weak
Ⓖ ill
Ⓗ strong
Ⓙ intelligent

5. Ⓐ work
Ⓑ roam
Ⓒ write
Ⓓ journey

6. Ⓕ hostage
Ⓖ relative
Ⓗ prisoner
Ⓙ partner

7. Ⓐ a guard
Ⓑ a servant
Ⓒ an athlete
Ⓓ a clerk

8. Ⓕ forgiven
Ⓖ encouraged
Ⓗ forbidden
Ⓙ taxed

9. Ⓐ a distraction
Ⓑ an order
Ⓒ an assignment
Ⓓ a cure

10. Ⓕ contained
Ⓖ infectious
Ⓗ rare
Ⓙ common

11. Ⓐ normal
Ⓑ dreary
Ⓒ outlandish
Ⓓ detailed

12. Ⓕ reversible
Ⓖ unchangeable
Ⓗ important
Ⓙ simple

13. Ⓐ heightened
Ⓑ decreased
Ⓒ simplified
Ⓓ diminished

14. Ⓕ expensive
Ⓖ enjoyable
Ⓗ thrifty
Ⓙ healthy

15. Ⓐ bright
Ⓑ gloomy
Ⓒ windy
Ⓓ changeable

16. Ⓕ escape from
Ⓖ cooperate with
Ⓗ work for
Ⓙ collide with

17. Ⓐ journey
Ⓑ reward
Ⓒ toy
Ⓓ story

GO ON

Name ____________________ Date ____________

**Sample B**

Ⓐ only in the tropics

Ⓑ only in the Arctic

Ⓒ in both the tropics and the Arctic

Ⓓ in neither the tropics nor the Arctic

STOP

**For questions 18–28, listen to the passage. Then darken the circle for the word or words that best answer the question.**

**18.** Ⓕ caught scarlet fever

Ⓖ invented the electric light

Ⓗ made improvements to the telephone

Ⓙ developed a research laboratory

**19.** Ⓐ invent the telegraph

Ⓑ worked on an electric generator

Ⓒ made sound recordings

Ⓓ found a cure for scarlet fever

**20.** Ⓕ 1847 into a wealthy family

Ⓖ 1847 into a poor family

Ⓗ 1847 into an immigrant family

Ⓙ 1847 into a middle-class family

**21.** Ⓐ an almanac

Ⓑ a sports magazine

Ⓒ a science or health book

Ⓓ a fantasy book

**22.** Ⓕ persuade people to send their teeth to a professor in Norway

Ⓖ present information

Ⓗ alarm people about pollution

Ⓙ warn people not to throw away their baby teeth

**23.** Ⓐ He sends it to environmental agencies.

Ⓑ He draws conclusions about pollution in different areas.

Ⓒ He writes a treatment plan for people who are ill.

Ⓓ He predicts illnesses people are likely to get.

**24.** Ⓕ he wanted to become famous

Ⓖ he wanted to meet new people

Ⓗ he was bored

Ⓙ the principal asked him to

**25.** Ⓐ speaking to the director

Ⓑ talking to the principal

Ⓒ asking other actors

Ⓓ on the school calendar

**26.** Ⓕ because the director asked him to

Ⓖ he wanted to stay busy

Ⓗ he had a great time being in the play

Ⓙ so he could keep his grades up

**27.** Ⓐ the local high school

Ⓑ the band and orchestra teachers

Ⓒ the PTA

Ⓓ the seventh- and eighth-grade bands and orchestras

**28.** Ⓕ all seventh graders

Ⓖ all eighth graders

Ⓗ seventh- and eighth-grade band and orchestra members

Ⓙ only eighth-grade band members

STOP

Name ______________________ Date ______________________

# Unit 13: Practice Test 5

You have 35 minutes to complete this test. Use the answer sheet on page 128 to mark your answers.

## LANGUAGE

**Sample A**

Ben wants to write a letter to his state senators expressing his opinion about the proposed building of a garbage dump in a wetlands area in his community. Before he writes the letter, he wants to find information about the location of wetlands areas in his state. He should look in —

Ⓐ a thesaurus.

Ⓑ the periodicals database at a library.

Ⓒ an atlas.

Ⓓ a dictionary.

STOP

**For questions 1–4, darken the circle for the correct answer, or write in your answer.**

Sheila was assigned to write a report about agriculture. She decided to research backyard gardening and use this as the subject of her report.

1. What should Sheila do before she writes her report?

______________________

______________________

______________________

2. Sheila wants to organize her thoughts for her report. Which of the following ideas should be grouped together with choosing a garden site?

Ⓐ explaining how to use fertilizer

Ⓑ testing soil for minerals and nutrients

Ⓒ weeding a garden

Ⓓ controlling plant disease

3. What would Sheila not want to include in her report?

Ⓕ a discussion of organic gardening methods

Ⓖ a chapter on pesticide use

Ⓗ a description of the types of fertilizers used in large farming operations

Ⓙ a list of plants grown by local backyard gardeners

4. Sheila wants to find information about the most recently developed hybrids of seeds. Where is the best place for Sheila to look to find this information?

Ⓐ an encyclopedia

Ⓑ her science textbook

Ⓒ a dictionary

Ⓓ the periodicals database at a library

GO ON

Name ______________________________ Date ______________

**Here are the Table of Contents and Index from books Sheila found on backyard gardening. Study them carefully. Then answer questions 5–9.**

**Book 1**

**Table of Contents**

| **Chapter** | **Page** |
|---|---|
| **1.** How To Choose a Site | 1 |
| **2.** Tools and Other Equipment | 8 |
| **3.** Preparing the Ground | 15 |
| **4.** What, When, and How To Plant | 21 |
| **5.** Caring for Your Plants | 23 |
| **6.** Controlling Pests in Your Garden | 27 |
| **7.** Harvesting | 32 |

**Book 2**

**Index**

Cabbage, 21–23
    harvesting, 32–33
    pest control, 27–29
Care of garden, 23–26; 27–31
    fertilizing, 15–17
    pest control, 27–31
    watering, 25
    weeding, 26
Carrots, 21–22
    planting tips, 22
    harvesting, 34
Cucumbers, 22, 25
    beetle control, 30
    planting tips, 22
Cutworms, control of, 29
Dandelions, 27
Drainage, 1–3
Fertilizers, 15–17
Frost dates, 22–23
Fungicides, 29

**5.** Sheila wanted to find information about growing carrots. All of these pages in Book 2 would be useful <u>except</u> —

Ⓕ 21
Ⓖ 22
Ⓗ 23
Ⓙ 34

**6.** Which chapter in Book 1 should Sheila read to find information about how to use a hoe when weeding a garden?

Ⓐ Chapter 1
Ⓑ Chapter 2
Ⓒ Chapter 3
Ⓓ Chapter 4

**7.** Which chapter in Book 1 should Sheila read to learn about controlling insects in the garden?

Ⓕ Chapter 3
Ⓖ Chapter 4
Ⓗ Chapter 5
Ⓙ Chapter 6

**8.** Sheila wanted to write a paragraph about choosing a garden site that had proper drainage. On which pages in Book 2 could she probably find the most useful information on this topic?

______________________________
______________________________
______________________________

**9.** Which pages in Book 2 would have information on the best time to plant cabbage?

______________________________
______________________________
______________________________

GO ON

Name ______________________________ Date ______________

**Here is a rough draft of the first part of Sheila's report. Read the rough draft carefully. Then answer questions 10–16.**

## Backyard Gardening

**(1)** How big is my backyard? **(2)** How much time do I have? **(3)** What kinds of vegetables, fruits, and flowers do I like? **(4)** How much space does each plant need to grow properly?

**(5)** Choosing a site for your garden requires you to identify several things. **(6)** First, you need to find an area that gets plenty of sunshine—about six hours of direct sunlight per day. **(7)** Second, the ground should be fairly level, with a slight slope for good drainage. **(8)** Finally, you need to check to make sure that the soil is free of rocks. **(9)** Third, you need a water source for watering your plants in dry weather.

**(10)** Once you have identified it, measure your site. **(11)** You need to find out the size of the site. **(12)** On paper, make a plan of your garden using the measurements. **(13)** Decide what kinds of plants you want to raise and where you will plant them. **(14)** Where you will plant them depends on many things. **(15)** For example, corn in front of beans. **(16)** When the corn grows tall, you don't want it to shade the beans from the sun. **(17)** You need to plant cucumbers along a fence or a trellis so the vines have a place to climb as they grow.

Name ________________________________ Date ____________

**10.** What is the best way to write sentence 6?

Ⓐ In the beginning, you need to find an area that gets plenty of sunshine—about six hours of direct sunlight per day.

Ⓑ About six hours of sunlight per day, is the first thing you need to find an area.

Ⓒ Once you need to find an area that gets plenty of sunshine—about six hours of direct sunlight per day.

Ⓓ As it is written.

**11.** Which of these sentences could be added after sentence 4?

Ⓕ What time do you usually go to bed at night?

Ⓖ These are questions you should ask yourself before you plan your backyard garden.

Ⓗ Backyard gardening is a worthwhile hobby.

Ⓙ What is your favorite sport in the summer?

**12.** Which sentence needlessly repeats an idea in the previous sentence?

Ⓐ 10

Ⓑ 11

Ⓒ 12

Ⓓ 13

**13.** Which sentence is <u>not</u> in the correct place in the report?

Ⓕ 5

Ⓖ 6

Ⓗ 7

Ⓙ 8

**14.** What is the best way to write sentence 10?

______________________________

______________________________

______________________________

______________________________

______________________________

**15.** Which group of words is <u>not</u> a complete sentence?

Ⓐ 13

Ⓑ 14

Ⓒ 15

Ⓓ 16

**16.** Which of these sentences could be added after sentence 17?

Ⓕ Your plants need water every day.

Ⓖ You should ask someone to water your plants if you go on vacation.

Ⓗ This allows the cucumbers to ripen in the full sun.

Ⓙ Fresh carrots from the garden taste good in salads.

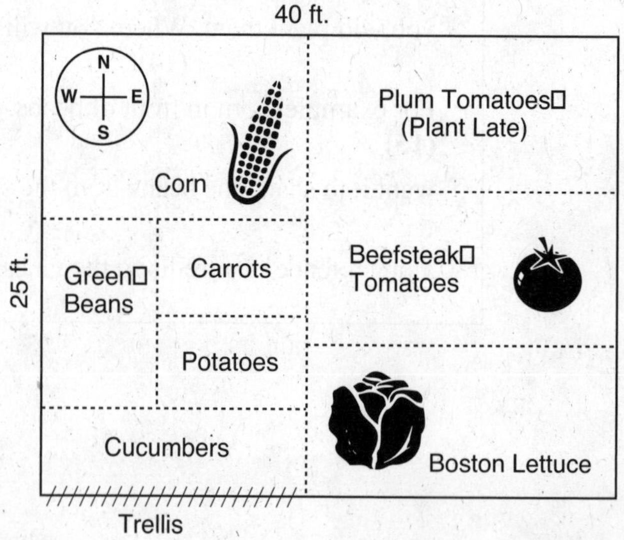

GO ON

Name ______________________________ Date ______________________

**Here is the next part of the rough draft of Sheila's report. This part has certain words and phrases underlined. Read the draft carefully. Then answer questions 17–24.**

**(18)** The proper tools for gardening helped make the job of caring for the garden less difficult. **(19)** Gardening tools can be bought at garage sales because they do not never need to be new to be effective. **(20)** The following tools are essential for gardening: a spade a metal rake a hoe wooden stakes string gardening gloves. **(21)** Some optional tools include a weeder and a cultivator.

**(22)** Tools must be cared for properly. **(23)** They, for example, should be cleaned with soap and water and dried with a clean rag. **(24)** Put the tools away, when not in use, in a storage shed, basement, or garage. **(25)** Lightly oil the tools once a month to keep it from rusting.

**(26)** You can use fertilizers, and watch your garden grow! **(27)** The United States Backyard Garden Club recommends using organic materials for the best-tasting vegetables. **(28)** A compost pile are made up of layers of grass clippings, leaves, vegetable peelings, and dead leaves and flowers. **(29)** These materials decay and become rich fertilizer without costing you any money. **(30)** Besides, you can never over-fertilize when using compost, and using compost helps keep excess fertilizer from running off into the water system.

GO ON

Name ______________________________ Date ______________

17. In sentence 18, helped is best written —

Ⓐ has helped

Ⓑ have helped

Ⓒ help

Ⓓ As it is written.

18. Correctly rewrite sentence 19.

______________________________

______________________________

______________________________

______________________________

19. Correctly rewrite sentence 20.

______________________________

______________________________

______________________________

______________________________

20. In sentence 23, They, for example, should is best written —

Ⓕ They, for example should

Ⓖ For example, they should

Ⓗ For example tools should

Ⓙ As it is written.

21. In sentence 25, it is best written —

Ⓐ them

Ⓑ they

Ⓒ their

Ⓓ As it is written.

22. In sentence 26, fertilizers, and watch is best written —

Ⓕ fertilizers and, watch

Ⓖ fertilizers and watch

Ⓗ fertilizers and watch,

Ⓙ As it is written.

23. In sentence 27, United States Backyard Garden Club is best written —

Ⓐ United States backyard Garden Club

Ⓑ United States Backyard Garden club

Ⓒ United States backyard garden club

Ⓓ As it is written.

24. In sentence 28, compost pile are made up is best written —

Ⓕ composts piles are made up

Ⓖ compost piles are made up

Ⓗ compost pile is made up

Ⓙ As it is written.

GO ON

Name ______________________ Date ______________

**For questions 25–36, read each sentence carefully. If one of the words is misspelled, darken the circle for that word. If all of the words are spelled correctly, then darken the circle for *No mistake*.**

**25.** The door mekanism is broken and we are locked out. No mistake
Ⓐ mekanism Ⓑ broken Ⓒ locked Ⓓ No mistake

**26.** He carryied the groceries up the stairs. No mistake
Ⓕ carryied Ⓖ groceries Ⓗ stairs Ⓙ No mistake

**27.** Carmen's vacuum cleaner motor burned out. No mistake
Ⓐ vacuum Ⓑ cleaner Ⓒ burned Ⓓ No mistake

**28.** It would be desireable if we could leave by midnight. No mistake
Ⓕ desireable Ⓖ leave Ⓗ midnight Ⓙ No mistake

**29.** The aluminum factory produces a great deal of polution. No mistake
Ⓐ aluminum Ⓑ produces Ⓒ polution Ⓓ No mistake

**30.** Rasberries grow best in temperate climates. No mistake
Ⓕ Rasberries Ⓖ temperate Ⓗ climates Ⓙ No mistake

**31.** Charles felt extremely week following his illness. No mistake
Ⓐ extremely Ⓑ week Ⓒ illness Ⓓ No mistake

**32.** We formed a semecircle around the park ranger. No mistake
Ⓕ formed Ⓖ semecircle Ⓗ ranger Ⓙ No mistake

**33.** She lives near the boarder between the two countries. No mistake
Ⓐ near Ⓑ boarder Ⓒ countries Ⓓ No mistake

**34.** The magician dissappeared right in front of our eyes. No mistake
Ⓕ magician Ⓖ dissappeared Ⓗ front Ⓙ No mistake

**35.** The collection of artifacts was quite inpressive. No mistake
Ⓐ collection Ⓑ artifacts Ⓒ inpressive Ⓓ No mistake

**36.** The bakeing bread created a pleasant aroma. No mistake
Ⓕ bakeing Ⓖ pleasant Ⓗ aroma Ⓙ No mistake

STOP

# Answer Sheet for Students

| STUDENT'S NAME | | | | | | | | | | | | | | | | | |
|---|---|---|---|---|---|---|---|---|---|---|---|---|---|---|---|---|---|
| LAST | | | | | | | | | | | FIRST | | | | | | MI |
| | | | | | | | | | | | | | | | | | |
| ○ | ○ | ○ | ○ | ○ | ○ | ○ | ○ | ○ | ○ | ○ | ○ | ○ | ○ | ○ | ○ | ○ | ○ |
| A | A | A | A | A | A | A | A | A | A | A | A | A | A | A | A | A | A |
| B | B | B | B | B | B | B | B | B | B | B | B | B | B | B | B | B | B |
| C | C | C | C | C | C | C | C | C | C | C | C | C | C | C | C | C | C |
| D | D | D | D | D | D | D | D | D | D | D | D | D | D | D | D | D | D |
| E | E | E | E | E | E | E | E | E | E | E | E | E | E | E | E | E | E |
| F | F | F | F | F | F | F | F | F | F | F | F | F | F | F | F | F | F |
| G | G | G | G | G | G | G | G | G | G | G | G | G | G | G | G | G | G |
| H | H | H | H | H | H | H | H | H | H | H | H | H | H | H | H | H | H |
| I | I | I | I | I | I | I | I | I | I | I | I | I | I | I | I | I | I |
| J | J | J | J | J | J | J | J | J | J | J | J | J | J | J | J | J | J |
| K | K | K | K | K | K | K | K | K | K | K | K | K | K | K | K | K | K |
| L | L | L | L | L | L | L | L | L | L | L | L | L | L | L | L | L | L |
| M | M | M | M | M | M | M | M | M | M | M | M | M | M | M | M | M | M |
| N | N | N | N | N | N | N | N | N | N | N | N | N | N | N | N | N | N |
| O | O | O | O | O | O | O | O | O | O | O | O | O | O | O | O | O | O |
| P | P | P | P | P | P | P | P | P | P | P | P | P | P | P | P | P | P |
| Q | Q | Q | Q | Q | Q | Q | Q | Q | Q | Q | Q | Q | Q | Q | Q | Q | Q |
| R | R | R | R | R | R | R | R | R | R | R | R | R | R | R | R | R | R |
| S | S | S | S | S | S | S | S | S | S | S | S | S | S | S | S | S | S |
| T | T | T | T | T | T | T | T | T | T | T | T | T | T | T | T | T | T |
| U | U | U | U | U | U | U | U | U | U | U | U | U | U | U | U | U | U |
| V | V | V | V | V | V | V | V | V | V | V | V | V | V | V | V | V | V |
| W | W | W | W | W | W | W | W | W | W | W | W | W | W | W | W | W | W |
| X | X | X | X | X | X | X | X | X | X | X | X | X | X | X | X | X | X |
| Y | Y | Y | Y | Y | Y | Y | Y | Y | Y | Y | Y | Y | Y | Y | Y | Y | Y |
| Z | Z | Z | Z | Z | Z | Z | Z | Z | Z | Z | Z | Z | Z | Z | Z | Z | Z |

SCHOOL:

TEACHER:

FEMALE ○ MALE ○

| BIRTH DATE | | | | |
|---|---|---|---|---|
| MONTH | DAY | | YEAR | |
| Jan ○ | 0 | 0 | 0 | 0 |
| Feb ○ | 1 | 1 | 1 | 1 |
| Mar ○ | 2 | 2 | 2 | 2 |
| Apr ○ | 3 | 3 | 3 | 3 |
| May ○ | | 4 | 4 | 4 |
| Jun ○ | | 5 | 5 | 5 |
| Jul ○ | | 6 | 6 | 6 |
| Aug ○ | | 7 | 7 | 7 |
| Sep ○ | | 8 | 8 | 8 |
| Oct ○ | | 9 | 9 | 9 |
| Nov ○ | | | | |
| Dec ○ | | | | |

GRADE ④ ⑤ ⑥ ⑦ ⑧

**Core Skills: Test Preparation**

**Grade 8**

**Fill in the circle for each multiple-choice answer. Write the answers to the open-ended questions on a separate sheet of paper.**

---

**TEST 1 Reading Comprehension**

SA Ⓐ Ⓑ Ⓒ Ⓓ
1. Ⓐ Ⓑ Ⓒ Ⓓ
2. Ⓕ Ⓖ Ⓗ Ⓙ
3. Ⓐ Ⓑ Ⓒ Ⓓ
4. Ⓕ Ⓖ Ⓗ Ⓙ
5. Ⓐ Ⓑ Ⓒ Ⓓ
6. Ⓕ Ⓖ Ⓗ Ⓙ
7. OPEN ENDED
8. OPEN ENDED
9. Ⓐ Ⓑ Ⓒ Ⓓ
10. Ⓕ Ⓖ Ⓗ Ⓙ
11. Ⓐ Ⓑ Ⓒ Ⓓ
12. Ⓕ Ⓖ Ⓗ Ⓙ
13. Ⓐ Ⓑ Ⓒ Ⓓ
14. Ⓕ Ⓖ Ⓗ Ⓙ
15. Ⓐ Ⓑ Ⓒ Ⓓ
16. Ⓕ Ⓖ Ⓗ Ⓙ
17. Ⓐ Ⓑ Ⓒ Ⓓ
18. OPEN ENDED
19. Ⓕ Ⓖ Ⓗ Ⓙ
20. Ⓐ Ⓑ Ⓒ Ⓓ
21. Ⓕ Ⓖ Ⓗ Ⓙ
22. Ⓐ Ⓑ Ⓒ Ⓓ
23. Ⓕ Ⓖ Ⓗ Ⓙ
24. OPEN ENDED
25. Ⓐ Ⓑ Ⓒ Ⓓ
26. OPEN ENDED

---

**TEST 2 Reading Vocabulary**

SA Ⓐ Ⓑ Ⓒ Ⓓ
1. Ⓐ Ⓑ Ⓒ Ⓓ
2. Ⓕ Ⓖ Ⓗ Ⓙ
3. Ⓐ Ⓑ Ⓒ Ⓓ
4. Ⓕ Ⓖ Ⓗ Ⓙ
5. Ⓐ Ⓑ Ⓒ Ⓓ
6. Ⓕ Ⓖ Ⓗ Ⓙ
7. Ⓐ Ⓑ Ⓒ Ⓓ
8. Ⓕ Ⓖ Ⓗ Ⓙ
9. Ⓐ Ⓑ Ⓒ Ⓓ

SB Ⓐ Ⓑ Ⓒ Ⓓ
10. Ⓕ Ⓖ Ⓗ Ⓙ
11. Ⓐ Ⓑ Ⓒ Ⓓ
12. Ⓕ Ⓖ Ⓗ Ⓙ
13. Ⓐ Ⓑ Ⓒ Ⓓ
14. Ⓕ Ⓖ Ⓗ Ⓙ

SC Ⓐ Ⓑ Ⓒ Ⓓ
15. Ⓐ Ⓑ Ⓒ Ⓓ
16. Ⓕ Ⓖ Ⓗ Ⓙ
17. Ⓐ Ⓑ Ⓒ Ⓓ
18. Ⓕ Ⓖ Ⓗ Ⓙ
19. Ⓐ Ⓑ Ⓒ Ⓓ
20. Ⓕ Ⓖ Ⓗ Ⓙ
21. Ⓐ Ⓑ Ⓒ Ⓓ
22. Ⓕ Ⓖ Ⓗ Ⓙ

# Answer Sheet for Students (cont.)

**TEST 3** **Part 1: Math Problem Solving**

| SA Ⓐ Ⓑ Ⓒ Ⓓ | 8. Ⓐ Ⓑ Ⓒ Ⓓ | 16. OPEN ENDED | 24. Ⓐ Ⓑ Ⓒ Ⓓ | 32. Ⓕ Ⓖ Ⓗ Ⓙ | 40. Ⓐ Ⓑ Ⓒ Ⓓ |
|---|---|---|---|---|---|
| 1. Ⓐ Ⓑ Ⓒ Ⓓ | 9. Ⓕ Ⓖ Ⓗ Ⓙ | 17. Ⓐ Ⓑ Ⓒ Ⓓ | 25. OPEN ENDED | 33. Ⓐ Ⓑ Ⓒ Ⓓ | 41. Ⓕ Ⓖ Ⓗ Ⓙ |
| 2. OPEN ENDED | 10. Ⓐ Ⓑ Ⓒ Ⓓ | 18. Ⓕ Ⓖ Ⓗ Ⓙ | 26. Ⓕ Ⓖ Ⓗ Ⓙ | 34. Ⓕ Ⓖ Ⓗ Ⓙ | 42. Ⓐ Ⓑ Ⓒ Ⓓ |
| 3. Ⓕ Ⓖ Ⓗ Ⓙ | 11. Ⓕ Ⓖ Ⓗ Ⓙ | 19. OPEN ENDED | 27. Ⓐ Ⓑ Ⓒ Ⓓ | 35. OPEN ENDED | 43. OPEN ENDED |
| 4. Ⓐ Ⓑ Ⓒ Ⓓ | 12. Ⓐ Ⓑ Ⓒ Ⓓ | 20. Ⓐ Ⓑ Ⓒ Ⓓ | 28. Ⓕ Ⓖ Ⓗ Ⓙ | 36. Ⓐ Ⓑ Ⓒ Ⓓ | 44. Ⓕ Ⓖ Ⓗ Ⓙ |
| 5. Ⓕ Ⓖ Ⓗ Ⓙ | 13. Ⓕ Ⓖ Ⓗ Ⓙ | 21. Ⓕ Ⓖ Ⓗ Ⓙ | 29. Ⓐ Ⓑ Ⓒ Ⓓ | 37. Ⓕ Ⓖ Ⓗ Ⓙ | 45. Ⓐ Ⓑ Ⓒ Ⓓ |
| 6. Ⓐ Ⓑ Ⓒ Ⓓ | 14. Ⓐ Ⓑ Ⓒ Ⓓ | 22. OPEN ENDED | 30. Ⓕ Ⓖ Ⓗ Ⓙ | 38. Ⓐ Ⓑ Ⓒ Ⓓ | 46. Ⓕ Ⓖ Ⓗ Ⓙ |
| 7. Ⓕ Ⓖ Ⓗ Ⓙ | 15. Ⓕ Ⓖ Ⓗ Ⓙ | 23. OPEN ENDED | 31. Ⓐ Ⓑ Ⓒ Ⓓ | 39. Ⓕ Ⓖ Ⓗ Ⓙ | 47. OPEN ENDED |

**TEST 3** **Part 2: Math Procedures**

| SA Ⓐ Ⓑ Ⓒ Ⓓ Ⓔ | 3. Ⓐ Ⓑ Ⓒ Ⓓ Ⓔ | 7. Ⓐ Ⓑ Ⓒ Ⓓ Ⓔ | 11. OPEN ENDED |
|---|---|---|---|
| SB Ⓕ Ⓖ Ⓗ Ⓙ Ⓚ | 4. Ⓕ Ⓖ Ⓗ Ⓙ Ⓚ | 8. Ⓕ Ⓖ Ⓗ Ⓙ Ⓚ | 12. OPEN ENDED |
| 1. Ⓐ Ⓑ Ⓒ Ⓓ Ⓔ | 5. Ⓐ Ⓑ Ⓒ Ⓓ Ⓔ | 9. Ⓐ Ⓑ Ⓒ Ⓓ Ⓔ | 13. Ⓐ Ⓑ Ⓒ Ⓓ Ⓔ |
| 2. Ⓕ Ⓖ Ⓗ Ⓙ Ⓚ | 6. Ⓕ Ⓖ Ⓗ Ⓙ Ⓚ | 10. Ⓕ Ⓖ Ⓗ Ⓙ Ⓚ | 14. Ⓕ Ⓖ Ⓗ Ⓙ Ⓚ |

**TEST 4** **Listening**

| SA Ⓐ Ⓑ Ⓒ Ⓓ | 5. Ⓐ Ⓑ Ⓒ Ⓓ | 10. Ⓕ Ⓖ Ⓗ Ⓙ | 15. Ⓐ Ⓑ Ⓒ Ⓓ | 19. Ⓐ Ⓑ Ⓒ Ⓓ | 24. Ⓕ Ⓖ Ⓗ Ⓙ |
|---|---|---|---|---|---|
| 1. Ⓐ Ⓑ Ⓒ Ⓓ | 6. Ⓕ Ⓖ Ⓗ Ⓙ | 11. Ⓐ Ⓑ Ⓒ Ⓓ | 16. Ⓕ Ⓖ Ⓗ Ⓙ | 20. Ⓕ Ⓖ Ⓗ Ⓙ | 25. Ⓐ Ⓑ Ⓒ Ⓓ |
| 2. Ⓕ Ⓖ Ⓗ Ⓙ | 7. Ⓐ Ⓑ Ⓒ Ⓓ | 12. Ⓕ Ⓖ Ⓗ Ⓙ | 17. Ⓐ Ⓑ Ⓒ Ⓓ | 21. Ⓐ Ⓑ Ⓒ Ⓓ | 26. Ⓕ Ⓖ Ⓗ Ⓙ |
| 3. Ⓐ Ⓑ Ⓒ Ⓓ | 8. Ⓕ Ⓖ Ⓗ Ⓙ | 13. Ⓐ Ⓑ Ⓒ Ⓓ | SB Ⓐ Ⓑ Ⓒ Ⓓ | 22. Ⓕ Ⓖ Ⓗ Ⓙ | 27. Ⓐ Ⓑ Ⓒ Ⓓ |
| 4. Ⓕ Ⓖ Ⓗ Ⓙ | 9. Ⓐ Ⓑ Ⓒ Ⓓ | 14. Ⓕ Ⓖ Ⓗ Ⓙ | 18. Ⓕ Ⓖ Ⓗ Ⓙ | 23. Ⓐ Ⓑ Ⓒ Ⓓ | 28. Ⓕ Ⓖ Ⓗ Ⓙ |

**TEST 5** **Language**

| SA Ⓐ Ⓑ Ⓒ Ⓓ | 7. Ⓕ Ⓖ Ⓗ Ⓙ | 14. OPEN ENDED | 21. Ⓐ Ⓑ Ⓒ Ⓓ | 28. Ⓕ Ⓖ Ⓗ Ⓙ | 35. Ⓐ Ⓑ Ⓒ Ⓓ |
|---|---|---|---|---|---|
| 1. OPEN ENDED | 8. OPEN ENDED | 15. Ⓐ Ⓑ Ⓒ Ⓓ | 22. Ⓕ Ⓖ Ⓗ Ⓙ | 29. Ⓐ Ⓑ Ⓒ Ⓓ | 36. Ⓕ Ⓖ Ⓗ Ⓙ |
| 2. Ⓐ Ⓑ Ⓒ Ⓓ | 9. OPEN ENDED | 16. Ⓕ Ⓖ Ⓗ Ⓙ | 23. Ⓐ Ⓑ Ⓒ Ⓓ | 30. Ⓕ Ⓖ Ⓗ Ⓙ | |
| 3. Ⓕ Ⓖ Ⓗ Ⓙ | 10. Ⓐ Ⓑ Ⓒ Ⓓ | 17. Ⓐ Ⓑ Ⓒ Ⓓ | 24. Ⓕ Ⓖ Ⓗ Ⓙ | 31. Ⓐ Ⓑ Ⓒ Ⓓ | |
| 4. Ⓐ Ⓑ Ⓒ Ⓓ | 11. Ⓕ Ⓖ Ⓗ Ⓙ | 18. OPEN ENDED | 25. Ⓐ Ⓑ Ⓒ Ⓓ | 32. Ⓕ Ⓖ Ⓗ Ⓙ | |
| 5. Ⓕ Ⓖ Ⓗ Ⓙ | 12. Ⓐ Ⓑ Ⓒ Ⓓ | 19. OPEN ENDED | 26. Ⓕ Ⓖ Ⓗ Ⓙ | 33. Ⓐ Ⓑ Ⓒ Ⓓ | |
| 6. Ⓐ Ⓑ Ⓒ Ⓓ | 13. Ⓕ Ⓖ Ⓗ Ⓙ | 20. Ⓕ Ⓖ Ⓗ Ⓙ | 27. Ⓐ Ⓑ Ⓒ Ⓓ | 34. Ⓕ Ⓖ Ⓗ Ⓙ | |

# Core Skills: Test Preparation, Grade 8

## ANSWER KEY

**Unit 2: Page 7**
1. D
2. F
3. C
4. F

**Page 8**
1. A
2. H
3. large or roomy

**Page 9**
1. D
2. H
3. ancient 2-wheeled horse-drawn vehicles

**Page 10**
1. C
2. F
3. city

**Pages 11–12**
1. C
2. G
3. D
4. exercised; listened to his doctors; worked hard
5. B
6. H
7. C
8. The hop, step, and jump was dropped from the list of events in 1906.

**Page 13**
1. B
2. F
3. B
4. They are curved like a plane's wings and are flat on the bottom.

**Page 14**
1. B
2. H
3. B
4. Nick made sure that he had all the pieces required before he began assembling the model.

**Page 15**
1. D
2. J
3. This story mainly talks about how the Marines used Navajo as a code.

**Page 16**
1. C
2. G
3. The main idea is that dogs are useful.

**Pages 17–18**
1. B
2. Aspirin started as a trademark and became a common name.
3. G
4. C
5. Acrophobics fear more than falling.

**Page 19**
1. B
2. H
3. C
4. Typists were slowed down by the arrangement of the keys.

**Page 20**
1. C
2. F
3. C
4. The entire country was urged to have polio vaccinations.

**Pages 21–22**
1. C
2. Intermarriages created two new groups–mestizos and mulattos.
3. G
4. B

**Page 23**
1. D
2. F
3. Janna was an honest person.

**Page 24**
1. A
2. G
3. C

**Page 25**
1. A
2. J
3. D
4. The thieves were squirrels and chipmunks.

**Page 26**
1. The setting is a carousel.
2. C
3. F
4. C
5. The overall mood is one of darkness and sorrow.

**Page 27**
1. A
2. F
3. A
4. The author thinks that they provide fun family entertainment.

**Page 28**
1. B
2. We need to pass laws to control the amount of money people spend running for Congress.
3. J
4. The author blames the press.

**Page 29**
1. A
2. F
3. B
4. J

**Page 30**
1. B
2. He became more sure of himself.
3. H
4. The book sold very well and she was able to pay off her debts.

**Unit 3: Pages 31–40**
**Sample A:** D
1. B
2. G
3. D
4. F
5. A
6. H
7. B
8. G
9. First sentence.
10. Anger
11. C
12. H
13. A
14. H
15. B
16. G
17. B
18. H
19. B
20. He was having trouble reading.
21. let other students know about the library's programs
22. J
23. B
24. H
25. C
26. F
27. D
28. F
29. D
30. The last journal entry describes Queen Victoria Park.
31. Answers will vary.
32. F
33. C
34. G
35. D
36. G
37. It is the only dog food that protects against heartworm.
38. B
39. G
40. B
41. "The First Heart Surgeon"

**Test, pages 41–48**
**Sample A:** D
1. B
2. F
3. This article is about using little-known plants to solve the world's food problems.
4. A
5. F
6. B
7. He leaped onto the stairway.
8. G
9. D
10. F
11. Ballonets help maintain the shape of the envelope.
12. C
13. G
14. A
15. J
16. B
17. J
18. As the human population grows, more forests are cut down to make farms.
19. A
20. H
21. C
22. H
23. C
24. G
25. B
26. J
27. B
28. Most ingredients are cool vegetables.
29. H
30. There was a shortage of paper during World War I.
31. B
32. G

**Unit 4: Page 49**
**Sample A:** D
1. C
2. J
3. C
4. J
5. C
6. F
7. C
8. F
9. C
10. F

**Page 50**
**Sample A:** B
1. D
2. F
3. D
4. H

**Page 51**
**Sample A:** D
1. B
2. H
3. D
4. G
5. B
6. F
7. C
8. F

**Test, pages 52–54**
**Sample A:** B
1. C
2. J
3. C
4. J
5. A
6. H
7. D
8. F
9. smell

**Sample B:** B
10. A
11. J
12. D
13. J
14. A

**Sample C:** A
15. F
16. B
17. F
18. C
19. J
20. C
21. villain
22. clean

**Unit 5: Page 56**

**Problem 1**

**Step 1:** To determine if $50 is enough money for Migdalia's transportation for one week.

**Step 2:** She takes a bus twice a day, 3 days a week. The bus costs $48 for 10 one-way trips.

She drives 2 days a week. The car costs $.30 per mile. She drives 52 miles a day.

**Step 3:** Compute Migdalia's travel expenses for one week. Compare that value to $50.

**Step 4:** three days on a bus: $4.80 per trip ¥ 6 trips = $28.80

two days in car: $15.60 per day ¥ 2 days = $31.20

total for one week:

$$28.80
+ $31.20
$60.00

Migdalia has not set aside enough money.

**Step 5:** Yes, because $60 is the amount of money she needs, and she has only set aside $50.

**Page 57**

**Step 1:** To estimate what percent of the carpet will be left over.

**Step 2:** Alberto purchased 30 square yards of carpeting. 1 square yard = 9 square feet.

**Step 3:** Determine the number of square feet in 30 square yards. Compute the amount of carpeting needed for the room in square feet. Compute the amount of left over carpeting. Estimate what percent of the carpeting purchased is left over.

**Step 4:** Area of carpeting purchased (30 sq. yds.) = 270 sq. ft. Area of room = 240 sq. ft.

Amount of carpeting left over = 30 sq. ft.

$$\begin{array}{r} 270 \text{ sq. ft.} \\ -\ 240 \text{ sq. ft.} \\ \hline 30 \text{ sq. ft.} \end{array}$$

Approximately 10% of the carpeting purchased will be left over.

**Step 5:** Yes, because the computations are correct and the reasoning is sound.

**Unit 6: Pages 58–59**
**Sample A:** A
1. D
2. H
3. A
4. G
5. C
6. 2°
7. G
8. B
9. H
10. C
11. H

**Page 60**
**Sample A:** D
1. A
2. J
3. D
4. 12 c = 2,700
5. F

**Page 61**
**Sample A:** B
1. 56, 80
2. D
3. G

**Pages 62–63**
**Sample A:** B
1. A
2. H
3. A
4. J
5. C
6. 4
7. 225

**Pages 64–65**
**Sample A:** D
1. A
2. G
3. A
4. 400 $cm^3$
5. J
6. B
7. G
8. A
9. 94.2 inches

**Page 66**
**Sample A:** B
1. C
2. H
3. 250 kilometers

**Page 67**
**Sample A:** B
1. B
2. G
3. D
4. H
5. D
6. G

**Pages 68–69**
**Sample A:** D
1. D
2. J
3. B
4. March 9
5. G
6. B
7. 8
8. 12
9. F
10. C
11. J

**Page 70**
**Sample A:** D
1. B
2. H
3. A
4. K
5. C
6. J

**Pages 71–72**
**Sample A:** D
1. A
2. 4
3. B
4. H
5. F
6. E
7. H
8. C
9. F
10. $63.70

**Test 1, pages 73–79**
**Sample A:** B
1. D
2. H
3. A
4. H
5. B
6. F
7. A
8. F
9. B
10. F
11. D
12. H
13. D
14. F
15. $1,050
16. 43
17. B
18. H
19. 54, 81
20. 440
21. C
22. J
23. A
24. 25
25. J
26. B
27. J
28. C
29. 5
30. 160 cubic inches
31. G
32. A
33. G
34. D
35. J
36. C
37. F
38. Oakley and Starr
39. D
40. J
41. C
42. G
43. A
44. F
45. $134

**Test 2, pages 80–81**
**Sample A:** B
**Sample B:** J
1. A
2. H
3. B
4. F
5. C
6. K
7. B
8. $\frac{1}{8}$ or 0.125
9. H
10. C
11. G
12. D
13. F
14. $12,600

**Unit 7: Page 82**
**Sample A:** C
1. B
2. H
3. B
4. J
5. A
6. G
7. C
8. F
9. D
10. J

**Page 83**
**Sample A:** B
1. B
2. F
3. B
4. H
5. D
6. H
7. B
8. H
9. B
10. G

**Test, pages 84–85**
**Sample A:** D
1. A
2. G
3. A
4. H
5. D
6. J
7. C
8. F
9. B
10. J
11. A
12. H
13. A

**Sample B:** A
14. H
15. A
16. G
17. D
18. J
19. A
20. H
21. B
22. F
23. B
24. H

**Unit 8: Pages 86–90**
**Sample A:** A
1. B
2. F
3. D
4. Yesterday, Justin collapsed while running the mile in physical education class.
5. H
6. B
7. I was out of breath, and my lungs were in extreme pain.
8. F
9. C
10. G
11. C
12. F
13. D
14. G
15. C
16. J
17. B

**Page 91**
**Sample A:** B
1. B
2. G
3. A
4. F
5. B
6. H
7. D
8. H

**Test, pages 92–97**
**Sample A:** B
1. B
2. J
3. C
4. Answers will vary.
5. F
6. The Impressionists made an effort not to paint what they knew or felt about the subject-just what they saw.
7. D
8. H
9. D
10. J
11. From an early age, she was interested in painting.
12. studied art
13. D
14. J
15. A
16. F
17. B
18. H
19. A
20. G
21. A
22. H
23. D
24. G
25. D
26. H
27. B
28. F
29. C
30. H

**Pages 98–125**
See pages 131 and 132 for the multiple-choice answers.

**Comprehensive Tests: Open-Ended Answers**

**Page 99**
7. An entomologist is a scientist who studies insects.
8. They eat insects that damage flowering and food plants.

**Page 101**
18. A piece of gum once helped solve a murder.

**Page 103**
24. sugar and vinegar
26. Sprinkle cheese on top of the cutlets.

**Page 107**
2. −3°

**Page 109**
16. 31; 33; 35; 37; 39; 41
19. 120

**Page 110**
22. 29 students
23. $2\frac{1}{2}$

**Page 111**
25. 20

**Page 112**
35. 12

**Page 114**
43. 100 days
47. 16

**Page 116**
11. $335
12. $63.75

**Page 119**
1. make a list of topics to include in her report

**Page 120**
8. Pages 1–3
9. Pages 21–23

**Page 122**
14. Once you have identified your site, you need to measure it.

**Page 124**
18. Gardening tools can be bought at garage sales because they do not need to be new to be effective.
19. …for gardening: a spade, a metal rake, a hoe, wooden stakes, string, and gardening gloves.

STUDENT'S NAME | SCHOOL:

LAST | FIRST | MI | TEACHER:

FEMALE ○ MALE ○

BIRTH DATE

| MONTH | DAY | YEAR |
|---|---|---|
| Jan ○ Feb ○ Mar ○ Apr ○ May ○ Jun ○ Jul ○ Aug ○ Sep ○ Oct ○ Nov ○ Dec ○ | 0–3, 0–9 | 0–9, 0–9 |

GRADE ④ ⑤ ⑥ ⑦ ⑧

ANSWER KEY

## Core Skills: Test Preparation
## Grade 8

**Fill in the circle for each multiple-choice answer. Write the answers to the open-ended questions on a separate sheet of paper.**

### TEST 1 Reading Comprehension

SA A **B** C D
1. **A** B C D
2. F G H **J**
3. **A** B C D
4. **F** G H J
5. **A** B C D
6. **F** G H J
7. OPEN ENDED
8. OPEN ENDED
9. A **B** C D
10. F **G** H J
11. A **B** C D
12. **F** G H J
13. A B **C** D
14. F G **H** J
15. A B **C** D
16. F **G** H J
17. A B C **D**
18. OPEN ENDED
19. F **G** H J
20. A B **C** D
21. F G **H** J
22. A **B** C D
23. F **G** H J
24. OPEN ENDED
25. A B C **D**
26. OPEN ENDED

### TEST 2 Reading Vocabulary

SA A **B** C D
1. A B C **D**
2. **F** G H J
3. A B C **D**
4. **F** G H J
5. A B C **D**
6. F **G** H J
7. A B **C** D
8. **F** G H J
9. A **B** C D

SB **A** B C D

10. F G **H** J
11. A B **C** D
12. F G H **J**
13. A B **C** D
14. F G **H** J

SC A B **C** D

15. A B **C** D
16. **F** G H J
17. A **B** C D
18. F G **H** J
19. A **B** C D
20. F **G** H J
21. A **B** C D
22. F G H **J**

## TEST 3 Part 1: Math Problem Solving

SA A **B** C D

1. A **B** C D
2. OPEN ENDED
3. F G **H** J
4. A B **C** D
5. F G **H** J
6. A B C **D**
7. F **G** H J
8. A **B** C D
9. F G **H** J
10. A **B** C D
11. F **G** H J
12. A **B** C D
13. F G **H** J
14. **A** B C D
15. F G H **J**
16. OPEN ENDED
17. A **B** C D
18. F **G** H J
19. OPEN ENDED
20. A **B** C D
21. F G H **J**
22. OPEN ENDED
23. OPEN ENDED
24. A **B** C D
25. OPEN ENDED
26. F G H **J**
27. A B C **D**
28. F G H **J**
29. A **B** C D
30. F **G** H J
31. A B C **D**
32. **F** G H J
33. **A** B C D
34. F G **H** J
35. OPEN ENDED
36. A B **C** D
37. F **G** H J
38. A B **C** D
39. F **G** H J
40. A **B** C D
41. **F** G H J
42. A **B** C D
43. OPEN ENDED
44. **F** G H J
45. A B C **D**
46. F G **H** J
47. OPEN ENDED

## TEST 3 Part 2: Math Procedures

SA A **B** C D E

SB F G H **J** K

1. **A** B C D E
2. **F** G H J K
3. A B **C** D E
4. F G H J **K**
5. A B C **D** E
6. F G H J **K**
7. A B C **D** E
8. F G **H** J K
9. **A** B C D E
10. F G H **J** K
11. OPEN ENDED
12. OPEN ENDED
13. A **B** C D E
14. F **G** H J K

## TEST 4 Listening

SA A B C **D**

1. **A** B C D
2. F **G** H J
3. A **B** C D
4. F G **H** J
5. **A** B C D
6. F G H **J**
7. **A** B C D
8. F G **H** J
9. **A** B C D
10. F **G** H J
11. A B **C** D
12. F **G** H J
13. **A** B C D
14. F G **H** J
15. A **B** C D
16. **F** G H J
17. A B C **D**

SB A B **C** D

18. **F** G H J
19. A B **C** D
20. F G H **J**
21. A B **C** D
22. F **G** H J
23. A **B** C D
24. F **G** H J
25. **A** B C D
26. F G **H** J
27. **A** B C D
28. F G **H** J

## TEST 5 Language

SA A B **C** D

1. OPEN ENDED
2. A **B** C D
3. F G **H** J
4. A B C **D**
5. F G **H** J
6. A **B** C D
7. F G H **J**
8. OPEN ENDED
9. OPEN ENDED
10. A B C **D**
11. F **G** H J
12. A **B** C D
13. F G H **J**
14. OPEN ENDED
15. A B **C** D
16. F G **H** J
17. A B **C** D
18. OPEN ENDED
19. OPEN ENDED
20. F **G** H J
21. **A** B C D
22. F **G** H J
23. A B C **D**
24. F G **H** J
25. **A** B C D
26. **F** G H J
27. A B C **D**
28. **F** G H J
29. A B **C** D
30. **F** G H J
31. A **B** C D
32. F **G** H J
33. A **B** C D
34. F **G** H J
35. A B **C** D
36. **F** G H J

# ANSWER KEY